THE INTERNATIONAL STYLE

THE INTERNATIONAL STYLE

HENRY-RUSSELL HITCHCOCK
AND
PHILIP JOHNSON

With a new foreword by Philip Johnson

W. W. Norton & Company
New York • London

The text of this book is composed in Bodoni Book
with the display set in Barer Bodoni Titling
Composition by ComCom, Inc.
Manufacturing by the Courier Companies.
Book design by Chris Welch

Library of Congress Cataloging-in-Publication Data
Hitchcock, Henry-Russell, 1903–
    The international style / Henry-Russell Hitchcock and Philip
Johnson ; with a new foreword by Philip Johnson.
        p.   cm.
    Includes index.
    1. International style (Architecture)   I. Johnson, Philip, 1906–
    II. Title
  NA682.I58H57   1995
  724'.6—dc20   94–34379

ISBN 0-393-03651-0

W.W. Norton & Company, Inc., 500 Fifth Avenue, New York, N.Y. 10110
W.W. Norton & Company Ltd., 10 Coptic Street, London WC1A 1PU

1 2 3 4 5 6 7 8 9 0

To Marga

Contents

A C K N O W L E D G E M E N T S

The photographs and the plans were for the most part provided by the architects themselves. Seventeen, however, were taken by or for the authors. The photograph of the Electrical Institute in Moscow was obtained from Bruno Taut; that of the Electrical Laboratory in Tokyo from R. J. Neutra. The plans of the houses at the Weissenhofsiedlung in Stuttgart come from the official Werkbund publication of the 1927 Exposition (Akad. Verlag Dr. Fr. Wedekind & Co., Stuttgart). To the architects, editors, and photographers who aided in gathering the material grateful acknowledgement is due, as also to those kind friends who have so often read and criticized the text. The assistance of Jan Ruhtenberg of Berlin and of Professor Agnes Rindge of Vassar College was particularly valuable.

THE
INTERNATIONAL
STYLE

FOREWORD TO THE 1995 EDITION

by Philip Johnson

Any book two generations old is going to be dated—most especially a critical book on architecture. Our text of *The International Style,* written sixty-three years ago, makes quaint reading today. The moral certainty of the three of us responsible for the direction of the book makes it sound preachy and schoolmarmish. It was a natural result considering the personalities involved: Alfred Barr, the son of a Presbyterian minister; Henry-Russell Hitchcock, whose home was a stone's throw from Plymouth Rock; and myself, the son of Calvinist parents. We knew what was right and we were very evangelical about it.

Barr and I had met in 1929 when he was a professor of art at

Wellesley and I was a Harvard student. We got to be good friends very quickly, and after just a few weeks, he asked me if I'd like to head the Department of Architecture and Design at the Museum of Modern Art, which had just been founded and where he was to be the director. I said I didn't know anything about architecture, but he said, "You will."

Barr introduced me to Hitchcock in Paris, in May 1930. Immediately, we three felt that the current new style was of vital interest to all of us, and we decided to tour Europe by car to look at it. Our trips together in 1930 and 1931 were an education to me. We had no itinerary except to go through cities, just plain looking. We went to the Bauhaus and all the usual places. In Brno, Czechoslovakia, though, we found a building that wasn't on anybody's list. As we drove along, we discussed the idea of mounting an exhibition devoted to the new architecture.

Of the three of us, Russell had the great eye. He was a supreme historian. The text of our book was his. Alfred was the resident ideologue and goad; he was the one who came up with the title of the exhibition, insisting on capitalizing "International Style." He was the one who shaped our thinking, who led the battle for "strict principles." Of course, he was very interested in abstract art—he brought up the connection between Mondrian and modern architecture, which we liked very much. I was still somewhat of a student at the time. Therefore, I was five times as enthusiastic and propagandistic as they were. I was more Catholic than the Pope.

Our trio became closer over the years culminating in the exhibition at the Museum of Modern Art in 1932. The exhibition—which occurred almost simultaneously with the book's publication—was a *succès d'estime.* From one side, Marxists and those interested in the social side of architecture objected to the emphasis on design and style. They did not believe in ART as a spring of human activity, but were interested only in technology and usefulness. From the other side, older architects ("older" because we were in our twenties) resented the emphasis on the slick, oversimplified boxiness of modern architecture—these simple-minded, white, no-character, anybody-can-do-it structures.

The International Style had a longer life, it seems to me now, than ever it deserved. The general public couldn't have cared less; Americans have never looked too much at architecture anyway. The newspaper and magazine media didn't care either. But even though comparatively few people came to the exhibition, its impact was huge in the architecture world. It caused endless discussions and fights within the profession, at places like the Architectural League. And it resulted in big teaching jobs at American universities for Mies van der Rohe and Walter Gropius. The exhibition established architecture in the art world's eyes. It made architecture a respectable endeavor.

Its influence on individual architects was lasting: Le Corbusier influenced Richard Meier, Mies influenced the Chicagoans, and the International Style in general helped shape the work of Sir Norman Foster and Sir Richard Rogers.

As far as my own work was concerned, I was a devoted disciple of Mies and of the Style. The Style lasted clearly through the 1950s, but then I got bored with it. My reaction was an anti-father one. Anti-Mies. Anti-Modern. I joined in with what Robert A. M. Stern and Robert Venturi were doing, putting forth the continuity of history as something that could be learned from. Being an historian first and an architect afterward, I found the idea appealing. I jumped at Venturi's book, *Complexity and Contradiction in Architecture,* in the early sixties. But I'm a jumper-arounder anyhow. I was interested in Schinkel, Classicism, and Ledoux before I was interested in modern architecture.

One of the points that the book made was a key one—that the Modern movement was a "style" similar to Gothic or Baroque, and it was that point which caused the objections from practicing architects. Did we then and do we even now practice a "style" of architecture? We architects today can well understand the objections to that word. What architect likes to have labels on his work like a government permit, or a scholarly category? Had I been a practicing architect then, even I would have objected.

But look back. Consider the *Weissenhofsiedlung* which is still recognized as a major event in the history of the twenties. Didn't Mies impose a "style" on the participants? All white stucco, all flat roofs, large, horizontal windows. The word "style" was not used but, interestingly enough, the restrictions were imposed not by an academic but by Mies, a practicing architect.

It is in the nature and duty of an historian or a taxonomist to label things to understand them. How otherwise to refer to groups or directions in the arts? Hitchcock the historian was doing his job.

Now with 20/20 hindsight, it seems crystal clear that what Russell wrote in 1931 was a history of the previous great decade, not a prescription for the next one. Hitchcock's happy metaphor in his 1966 foreword of the river running through a narrow gorge with force and turbulence is an accurate description of the twenties. Before and—goodness knows—after that, the river took many courses and slowed its pace.

It was, regardless of its problems, a remarkable book, and, especially with Hitchcock's afterwords of twenty years and thirty years later, it was a turning point in the history and theory of the architecture of 1922–32. Or, as Hitchcock wrote in his 1966 foreword: "At least, however, the book represents an account by young and enthusiastic contemporaries of the new architecture of the twenties at the moment when it had reached its peak of achievement at the opening of the next decade."

And, dear reader, please remember the last words of the book. They are aimed at you. "We have an architecture still." Yes, but architecture's hold as art on professional and public intent is as precarious as it was in 1932.

May 1994
New York City

FOREWORD TO THE 1966 EDITION

by Henry-Russell Hitchcock

In 1931 the Museum of Modern Art, an institution then only two years old and thus far devoted primarily to the presentation of the work of painters, planned its first architectural exhibition. The director, Alfred Barr, asked Philip Johnson and me to organize this event, which took place the following year. The work of Le Corbusier, Oud, Gropius, Mies van der Rohe and, by contrast, that of Wright occupied the principal place in the exhibition. But there was also work by other Americans, notably Hood, Howe & Lescaze and Neutra, and some forty architects all told, representing building of the day in fifteen countries. Concurrently with the exhibition we prepared *The International Style: Architecture since 1922.*

After thirty-three years—a third of a century—the authors of a once-topical work have no obligation to bring that work up to date in a revised edition. The book has for some time belonged to history, and the "Style" (which Alfred Barr in his Preface to the book capitalized, but which we in our text did not) has been universally recognized. Fifteen years ago I wrote an article for the *Architectural Record* called "The International Style Twenty Years After" (reprinted here on p. 243). It still seemed worthwhile then to quote many passages from the original text and to comment on them in the light of later developments in the pre-war and post-war years. In his famous Glass House of 1949, Philip Johnson had shortly before given notable evidence of the continuity of the Miesian aspect of the International Style, as other American architects were at that point also doing, especially Eero Saarinen and the Skidmore firm.

Since then in our different ways, he most strikingly in his buildings that for ten years now have been moving away from the International Style as we understood it in 1932, I in various writings—most definitively in the relevant chapters 22, 23 and 25 of *Architecture Nineteenth and Twentieth Centuries,* and in the Epilogue to the second edition of that book published in 1963—have offered the conclusion that the International Style is over. Since then two protagonists have died, first Oud and then Le Corbusier, the architect who had proceeded furthest beyond the original style of the 1920's, and two old masters still survive, Gropius and Mies van der Rohe.

I am inclined now to say of the book that it was less remarkable for what it said than for the point in time when we said it. Had we written it several years earlier—as I had my *Modern Architecture of 1929,* shortly after the new style had won acclaim, if not acceptance, with the Werkbund exposition at Stuttgart in 1927 and Le Corbusier's projects of 1927–28 in the competitions for the Palace of the League of Nations—the canon of executed works on which our designation of the style was based would have been seriously incomplete, for the two finest houses in the new style—Le Corbusier's Villa Savoye and Mies's Tugendhat house—would not yet have existed. Had we written it a few years later—quite aside from the political proscription of modern design after 1933 in Germany, where the new style had hitherto been most successful, and aside from the slowdown of building for economic reasons in France and Holland—we would have had to face various developments that were sharply changing the international picture. On the one hand there was the renewal of Frank Lloyd Wright's activity after almost a decade of desuetude, a renewal that actually began with his first project (1932) for the Willey house of 1934, though it was generally recognized only with the construction of Falling Water and the Johnson Wax offices, both begun in 1936. On the other hand there was the rise to international prominence of Aalto, associated particularly with his pavilion at the Paris Exposition of 1937.

Aalto, not Wright, is illustrated in the book, since he had already shifted from Swedish Neoclassicism to the International Style in the late 1920's. We were certainly aware, moreover, of the considerable difference between his sculpturally shaped supports in the press-room of the Turun Sanomat at Turku and the slim round or square *pilotis* so characteristic of Le Corbusier and the International Style designers generally. Thus by the mid-thirties the Style was effectively rivaled—or rejected—both by older and by younger architects during just those years when it was also spreading most widely through the western world. In 1932, for example, we illustrated in our book only one building from Japan and none from Latin America.

Critical readers have always noticed that even in 1932 we had difficulty fitting into our basic description of the style Mies's German Pavilion at the Barcelona Exposition of 1929, which was acclaimed then—and has been ever since, in spite of its early demolition—as perhaps the supreme example of architectural design of the decade of the twenties, Le Corbusier's Errazuris project (which we mistakenly believed to have been executed) and his de Mandrot house. Both the solid rubble walls proposed or executed in these houses of Le Corbusier and the absence of volumetric enclosure in Mies's pavilion were presented by us merely as exceptions to our three basic criteria of the International Style.

But although we were unaware of it, while we were writing Le Corbusier was going much further in the Swiss Hostel at the Cité Universitaire in Paris. Not only was rough rubble used in a bearing wall—and an external wall of irregular curvature at that—without the justification of utilizing local rustic resources, as in the Andes and on the Riviera, but the *pilotis* were no longer related to the internal structure of the dormitory wing above them and were of raw concrete and slightly sculptural section, heavy and massive rather than frail and linear like those he had used hitherto.

Neither in gathering material for the exhibition on which the book was based nor in writing the book did we intend to provide a collection of recipes for success with the new style nor a prognosis, much less a premature obituary. Actually, contrary to our intentions, it would seem that what we merely *described* was, to some extent, followed like a prescription since it offered a logical amalgam of the practice of three new leaders, Le Corbusier, Gropius and Mies, already generally accepted as such by the international avant-garde. Hindsight suggests that Holland might have been better—or also—represented by Rietveld than by

Oud, who withdrew from production in 1930 for some years because of illness. In any case, we seemed later not wholly unsuccessful as the prophets we had not aspired to be. That aspect of the book, however, is perhaps exaggerated in the article of 1951.

As to the obituary aspect: Who shall say, a generation after its heyday, when the International Style died? That it is over is today as clear as that the near-revolution it constituted remains the basis, now become traditional, of later modern architecture. But the lines that, after 1930, led to *our* present in the 1960's, like the lines that before the 1920's led—often rather indirectly—to the International Style, are clearer to everyone now than they could possibly have been in 1932 either as history of the near-past or prognosis for the near future.

If one thinks of the development of architecture in this century which is now two-thirds over (one need no longer specify "modern" architecture) as being somewhat like a rope or a strip of fabric, one can now see that many disparate strands special to such architects as Wright, Berlage, Wagner, Loos, Mackintosh, Perret, and Behrens were stretched and thinned, in some cases quite drastically, as they were woven or wound into the tight braid of the International Style after World War I. One can even recognize that some of these strands also retained some independence and continued, with varying degrees of vitality, alongside the International Style: the "organic architecture" of Wright, the Amsterdam School, German Expressionism, Scandinavian Empiricism, and even others. These survivals, which are by now to some extent revivals, have complicated the architectural scene increasingly in the last twenty years. They have also undoubtedly enriched it. Our book was written just after the tightened braid had existed long enough to be clearly recognizable in most of its aspects and just before the integrated fabric of architectural style began to loosen again or, as some would see it, to fray.

To change the metaphor, one might rather see the history of architecture in our century as a flowing stream, at first slow-moving, broad and free, and varied by many eddies and side-currents before 1920, but then confined in the twenties to a narrower channel, so that for a while it rushed forward, on the physicists' principle of the venturi, at almost revolutionary speed. By the early thirties the stream was certainly beginning to widen and meander again. Our book was written looking backward at the preceding ten years of relatively strait and rapid flow, for its subtitle was "Architecture since 1922."

Whether later posterity will see in those years of the formation and early *succès d'estime* of the International Style as crucial an episode as it then seemed to us who were, however humbly, a part of it, there is no way of knowing. Now that a younger generation of critics and historians is turning the light of scholarly research on the 1920's legends are being corrected; de Klerk, Mendelsohn, Häring, Böhm, and other individualists are being reassessed; and at least statistical recognition is given to the immense volume of architectural production of the 1920's that was untouched by the rising International Style. Even considering only the work of trained architects and engineers, some ninety-nine percent, I suppose, of buildings were barely touched by the new ideas, whether because of their designers' scorn of aesthetic considerations of any sort or because of most architects' retention of earlier, though not necessarily rigidly "traditional," architectural concepts.

I think we can accept that the International Style was no mere superficial movement, like the Manoeline or the Art Nouveau, for it was concerned with many, if not all, of the essentials of any architecture. But that the analogies with the Greek and the Gothic in which we and other writers of the time so freely indulged will stand up—or, indeed, have even thus far stood up—I must now doubt. At least, however, the book represents an account by young and enthusiastic contemporaries of the new architecture of the twenties at the moment when it had reached its peak of achievement at the opening of the next decade.

September 1965
Northampton, Massachusetts

PREFACE

by Alfred H. Barr, Jr.

M<small>r.</small> Hitchcock and Mr. Johnson have studied contemporary architecture with something of the scholarly care and critical exactness customarily expended upon Classical or Mediæval periods. This book presents their conclusions, which seem to me of extraordinary, perhaps of epoch-making, importance. For they have proven beyond any reasonable doubt, I believe, that there exists today a modern style as original, as consistent, as logical, and as widely distributed as any in the past. The authors have called it the International Style.

To many this assertion of a new style will seem arbitrary and dogmatic. For it has become almost customary among the more serious American and English writers on modern architecture to conclude their essays by remarking that we are in a "period of gestation", that we have not yet "arrived at a consistent style". Such a conclusion is plausible enough to one who drives down Fifth Avenue, walks through the annual circus of the Architectural League, or reads the somewhat superficial books and articles published in the United States.

This uncertainty of direction is clearly demonstrated by two recent magazine articles, one on European and one on American architecture. The first, called *New Building for the New Age,* is illustrated by photographs of six buildings supposedly representative of "what is happening in architecture on the continent of Europe". They include Saarinen's pre-War Railway Station at Helsingfors; the bizarre Expressionist Einstein Tower (1920) at Potsdam and a ponderous department store, both by Mendelsohn; Tengbom's Concert Hall at Stockholm with its portico of tall decagonal columns surmounted by Corinthian capitals; a school by Dudok, one of the more advanced members of the conservative Amsterdam group; and a theatrical Danish church façade derived from Hanseatic Gothic prototypes. Could we have added the Romanesquoid Stuttgart Railway Station, a cubistic house from the rue Mallet-Stevens, a concrete church by the brothers Perret, and the neo-Barocco-Romanesque Town Hall of Stockholm, we would have nearly a complete list of the modern European buildings most familiar to the American public and, we are forced to believe, most admired by the large majority of American architects.

Poets in Steel, a characteristic essay on modern American architecture, is as one might expect primarily concerned with skyscrapers, although one of Mr. Cram's churches is illustrated and Frank Lloyd Wright is mentioned only to be dismissed as a mere theorist. But skyscrapers are accepted as "one of the most magnificent developments of our times"—Romanesque, Mayan, Assyrian, Renaissance, Aztec, Gothic, and especially Modernistic—everything from the stainless steel gargoyles of the Chrysler Building to the fantastic mooring mast atop the Empire State. No wonder that some of us who have been appalled by this chaos turn with the utmost interest and expectancy to the International Style.

It should be made clear that the aesthetic qualities of the Style are the principal concern of the authors of this book. Mr. Hitchcock has written elsewhere on its history and has published studies of several leading modern architects.[1] He and Mr. Johnson have also made little attempt to present here the technical or sociological aspects of the style except in so far as they are related to problems of design. They admit, of course, the extreme importance of these factors, which are often stressed in the criticism of modern architecture to the practical exclusion of problems of design.

The distinguishing aesthetic principles of the International Style as laid down by the authors are three: emphasis upon volume—space enclosed by thin planes or surfaces as opposed to the suggestion of mass and solidity; regularity as opposed to symmetry or other kinds of obvious balance; and, lastly, dependence upon the intrinsic elegance of materials, technical perfection, and fine proportions, as opposed to applied ornament.

The section on functionalism should be, I feel, of especial interest to American architects and critics. Functionalism as a dominant principle reached its high water mark among the important modern European architects several years ago. As was to

[1]*Frank Lloyd Wright,* Paris, 1928; *Modern Architecture: Romanticism and Reintegration,* New York, 1929; *J. J. P. Oud,* Paris, 1931. Mr. Johnson has in preparation a monograph on Miës van der Rohe.

be expected, several American architects have only recently begun to take up the utility-and-nothing-more theory of design with ascetic zeal. They fail to realize that in spite of his slogan, the house as a *machine á habiter*, Le Corbusier is even more concerned with style than with convenient planning or plumbing, and that the most luxurious of modern German architects, Miës van der Rohe, has for over a year been the head of the Bauhaus school, having supplanted Hannes Meyer, a fanatical functionalist. "Post-Functionalism" has even been suggested as a name for the new Style, at once more precise and genetically descripitive than "International".

American skyscraper architects with cynical good humor have been willing to label their capricious façade ornament "functional"—"one function of the building is to please the client". We are asked to take seriously the architectural taste of real estate speculators, renting agents, and mortgage brokers! It is not surprising that the modern critic should feel more sympathy with the sound academic achievements of conservative contemporaries than with these modernistic impresarios. One can never forget the naive megalomania expressed in the remark of one of our best known "masters of the skyscraper". "What! You wouldn't include so-and-so among your important architects? Why, he's built over two hundred million dollars' worth!" (Poor Ictinus with his couple of temples! Poor Peruzzi with his handful of palaces!)

It is, then, from the commercially successful modernistic architects that we may expect the strongest opposition to the Style. For even more than the great styles of the past it requires restraint and discipline, the will to perfect as well as to invent. And this is contrary to the American cult of individualism, whether genuinely romantic, as in the case of Frank Lloyd Wright, or merely the result of the advertising value of a 1932 model. American nationalists will also oppose the Style as another European invasion. But Oud and Gropius are proud to consider Frank Lloyd Wright among their artistic ancestors, even though their emulation of his work belongs definitely to the past.

Nevertheless, the International Style has already gained signal victories in America as is proven by a glance at the illustration of the skyscraper by Howe and Lescase. George Howe was formerly a well-established traditional architect in Philadelphia. And a comparison in sequence of Raymond Hood's four famous skyscrapers tells its own story: the Tribune Tower, Chicago, followed by the Radiator Building (1924), New York, both of them luxuriantly wigged and bearded with applied Gothic; then the spectacular verticalism of the Daily News Building (1930), and finally the McGraw-Hill Building (1931), which is more in the Style than any other New York skyscraper. A superficial but more general influence of the Style may be seen in the rapid change from vertical to horizontal emphasis in much recent metropolitan building.

In Europe, too, one may recall how during recent years Peter Behrens, the dean of German architects, and Mendelsohn, once the most conspicuous of the Expressionists, have both gone over to the International Style. Even in Stockholm—that shrine for our architectural schools—Asplund, the designer of the neoclassic Town Library, astonished the world by his mastery of "post-functionalist" design in the building of the Stockholm Exposition two years ago.

A preface should doubtless direct the attention of the reader to the text. And as in this book the text itself is intended as an introduction to the illustrations, one need scarcely speak at length about them. The authors have spent nearly two years in assembling the photographic and documentary material from which the illustrations were chosen. They form a carefully selected anthology of the Style as it has developed in Germany, Holland and France, and spread throughout the world, extending from Finland to Italy, from England to Russia, and beyond to Japan and the United States.

I

INTRODUCTION

The Idea of Style

T he light and airy systems of construction of the Gothic cathedrals, the freedom and slenderness of their supporting skeleton, afford, as it were, a presage of a style that began to develop in the nineteenth century, that of metallic architecture. With the use of metal, and of concrete reinforced by metal bars, modern builders could equal the most daring feats of Gothic architects without endangering the solidity of the structure. In the conflict that obtains between the two elements of construction, solidity and open space, everything seems to show that the principle of free spaces will prevail, that the palaces and houses of the future will be flooded with air and light. Thus the formula popularized by Gothic architecture has a great future before it. Following on the revival of Græco-Roman architecture which prevailed from the sixteenth century to our own day, we shall see, with the

full application of different materials, a yet more enduring rebirth of the
Gothic style.

Salomon Reinach, APOLLO, 1904

Since the middle of the eighteenth century there have been recurrent attempts to achieve and to impose a controlling style in architecture such as existed in the earlier epochs of the past. The two chief of these attempts were the Classical Revival and the Mediæval Revival. Out of the compromises between these two opposing schools and the difficulties of reconciling either sort of revivalism with the new needs and the new methods of construction of the day grew the stylistic confusion of the last hundred years.

The nineteenth century failed to create a style of architecture because it was unable to achieve a general discipline of structure and of design in the terms of the day. The revived "styles" were but a decorative garment to architecture, not the interior principles according to which it lived and grew. On the whole the development of engineering in building went on regardless of the Classical or Mediæval architectural forms which were borrowed from the past. Thus the chaos of eclecticism served to give the very idea of style a bad name in the estimation of the first modern architects of the end of the nineteenth and the beginning of the twentieth century.

In the nineteenth century there was always not one style, but "styles," and the idea of "styles" implied a choice. The individualistic revolt of the first modern architects destroyed the prestige of the "styles," but it did not remove the implication that there was a possibility of choice between one æsthetic conception of design and another. In their reaction against revivalism these men sought rather to explore a great variety of free possibilities.

34

The result, on the whole, added to the confusion of continuing eclecticism, although the new work possessed a general vitality which the later revivalists had quite lost. The revolt from stylistic discipline to extreme individualism at the beginning of the twentieth century was justified as the surest issue from an impasse of imitation and sterility. The individualists decried submission to fixed æsthetic principles as the imposition of a dead hand upon the living material of architecture, holding up the failure of the revivals as a proof that the very idea of style was an unhealthy delusion.

Today the strict issue of reviving the styles of the distant past is no longer one of serious consequence. But the peculiar traditions of imitation and modification of the styles of the past, which eclecticism inherited from the earlier Classical and Mediæval Revivals, have not been easily forgotten. The influence of the past still most to be feared is that of the nineteenth century with its cheapening of the very idea of style. Modern architecture has nothing but the healthiest lessons to learn from the art of the further past, if that art be studied scientifically and not in a spirit of imitation. Now that it is possible to emulate the great styles of the past in their essence without imitating their surface, the problem of establishing one dominant style, which the nineteenth century set itself in terms of alternative revivals, is coming to a solution.

The idea of style, which began to degenerate when the revivals destroyed the disciplines of the Baroque, has become real and fertile again. Today a single new style has come into existence. The æsthetic conceptions on which its disciplines are based derive from the experimentation of the individualists. They and not the revivalists were the immediate masters of those who have created the new style. This contemporary style, which exists throughout the world, is unified and inclusive, not fragmentary and contradictory like so much of the production of the first generation of modern architects. In the last decade it has produced sufficient monuments of distinction to display its validity and its vitality. It may fairly be compared in significance with the styles of the past. In the handling of the problems of structure it is related to the Gothic, in the handling of the problems of design it is more akin to the Classical. In the preëminence given to the handling of function it is distinguished from both.

The unconscious and halting architectural developments of the nineteenth century, the confused and contradictory experimentation of the beginning of the twentieth, have been succeeded by a directed evolution. There is now a single body of discipline, fixed enough to integrate contemporary style as a reality and yet elastic enough to permit individual interpretation and to encourage general growth.

The idea of style as the frame of potential growth, rather than as a fixed and crushing mould, has developed with the recognition of underlying principles such as archæologists discern in the great styles of the past. The principles are few and broad. They are not mere formulas of proportion such as distinguish the Doric from the Ionic order; they are fundamental, like the organic verticality of the Gothic or the rhythmical symmetry of the Baroque. There is, first, a new conception of architecture as volume rather than as mass. Secondly, regularity rather than axial symmetry serves as the chief means of ordering design. These two principles, with a third proscribing arbitrary applied decoration, mark the productions of the international style. This new style is not international in the sense that the production of one country is just like that of another. Nor is it so rigid that the work of various leaders is not clearly distinguishable. The international style has become evident and definable only gradually as different innovators throughout the world have successfully carried out parallel experiments.

In stating the general principles of the contemporary style, in analysing their derivation from structure and their modification by function, the appearance of a certain dogmatism can hardly be avoided. In opposition to those who claim that a new style of architecture is impossible or undesirable, it is necessary to stress the coherence of the results obtained within the range of possibilities thus far explored. For the international style already exists in the present; it is not merely something the future may hold in store. Architecture is always a set of actual monuments, not a vague corpus of theory.

II

H I S T O R Y

The style of the twelfth and thirteenth century was the last before our own day to be created on the basis of a new type of construction. The break away from the High Gothic in the later Middle Ages was an æsthetic break without significant structural development. The Renaissance was a surface change of style generally coupled with actual regression in terms of structure. The Baroque and *a fortiori* the Romantic Age concerned themselves all but exclusively with problems of design. When a century ago new structural developments in the use of metal made their appearance they remained outside the art of architecture. The Crystal Palace at the London Exposition of 1851, Paxton's magnificent iron and glass construction, has far more in common with the architecture of our day than with that of its own. Ferroconcrete, to which the contemporary style owes so much, was invented in 1849. Yet it was at least fifty years before it first began to play a considerable part in architectural construction.

Metal had begun to be used incidentally in architecture before the end of the eighteenth century. Thenceforth it achieved a place of increasing importance, even in buildings of the most traditional design. Finally in the eighties it made possible the first skyscrapers. But on the whole the "arcades," the train sheds, the conservatories and the exhibition halls, of which the London Crystal Palace was the earliest and the finest, were adjuncts to, or substitutes for, conventional masonry buildings.

Behind the conventional story of nineteenth century revivals and eclecticism there are two further histories of architecture. One deals with the science of building alone. It traces the development of new engineering methods of construction and the gradual replacement of traditional masonry structure by successive innovations. The other history deals with the development of the art of architectural design regardless of specific imitations. Design was freed here and there from the control of the past. Some architects even sought novel forms and many aimed at a more direct expression of the new methods of construction. A new art of proportioning plane surfaces, a free study of silhouette, even a frank use of metal appear in the work of most of the leading nineteenth century architects. Soane in England, Schinkel and his followers in Germany, and Labrouste in France, were among these early precursors of modern architecture.

Within the Classical Revival there developed a new sense of design, purer and more rational than that of the Renaissance or the Baroque, yet not restricted merely to the purity and rationalism of the Greeks. Within the Mediæval Revival there grew up a body of doctrine, based on the practice of the builders of the Middle Ages, which foreshadowed the theories of our own day. There is not much to change today in the passage that has been quoted from Salomon Reinach's *Apollo*. As late as 1904 it was possible to conceive of modern architecture chiefly as a sort of renaissance of the Gothic. Yet it should be stressed that the relation of the modern style to the Gothic is ideological rather than visual, a matter of principle rather than a matter of practice. In design, indeed, the leading modern architects aim at Greek serenity rather than Gothic aspiration.

In writing on modern architecture some few years ago it was possible to accept that the individualists of the end of the nineteenth century and the beginning of the twentieth, who first broke consciously with the nominal discipline of the revivals, established tentatively a *New Tradition*. It appeared then as a sort of style in which the greatest common denominator of the various revivals was preserved and fused with the new science of building. Today it seems more accurate to describe the work of the older generation of architects as half-modern. Each architect broke in his own way with the immediate past, each sought in his own direction the positive elements which have been combined in the last decade. But there was no real stylistic integration until after the War.

The industrial architecture of Peter Behrens in Germany in the years before the War was already extremely simplified and regular. The effect of volume began to replace the traditional effect of mass. Otto Wagner, a decade earlier in Vienna, cultivated qualities of lightness and developed the plane surfaces of his architecture for their own sake. The Belgian Van de Velde experimented with continuity of surface, making much use of curves. Berlage at Amsterdam based his compositions on geometry and handled both old and new materials with unusual straightforwardness. In the constructions of Perret in France the use of fer-roconcrete led to a visible articulation of the supporting skeleton with the walls treated as mere screens between the posts. Thus in the different countries of Europe before the War the conceptions of the international style had come independently into existence. It remained for the younger generation to combine and crystallize the various æsthetic and technical results of the experimentation of their elders.

But it was in America that the promise of a new style appeared first and, up to the War, advanced most rapidly. Richardson in the seventies and eighties often went as far as did the next gener-ation on the Continent in simplification of design and in direct expression of structure. Following him, Root and Sullivan de-duced from steel skyscraper construction principles which have been modified but not essentially changed by later generations. Their work of the eighties and nineties in Chicago is still too little known. We have in America only a few commercial buildings of 1900 to compare with the radical steel and glass department stores of Europe; but these few are more notable than all the sky-scrapers of the following twenty-five years.

In the first decades of the new century Frank Lloyd Wright continued brilliantly the work of the Chicago school in other fields of architecture. He introduced many innovations, particu-larly in domestic building, quite as important as those of the Art Nouveau and Jugendstil in France and Germany. His open plan-ning broke the mould of the traditional house, to which Europe clung down to the War. He also was the first to conceive of ar-chitectural design in terms of planes existing freely in three di-mensions rather than in terms of enclosed blocks. Wagner, Behr-ens and Perret lightened the solid massiveness of traditional architecture; Wright dynamited it.

While much of the innovation in Europe merely consisted in

expressing more frankly new methods of construction within a framework of design still essentially Classical or Mediæval, Wright from the beginning was radical in his æsthetic experimentation. One may regret the lack of continuity in his development and his unwillingness to absorb the innovations of his contemporaries and his juniors in Europe. But one cannot deny that among the architects of the older generation Wright made more contributions than any other. His consciously novel ornament may appear to lack even the vitality of the semi-traditional ornament of the first quarter of the century in Europe. Perret was, perhaps, a more important innovator in construction; Van de Velde showed a greater consistency and a purer taste in his æsthetic experiments. But Wright preserved better the balance between the mere expression of structure and the achievement of positive form.

There is, however, a definite breach between Wright and the younger architects who created the contemporary style after the War. Ever since the days when he was Sullivan's disciple, Wright has remained an individualist. A rebel by temperament, he has refused even the disciplines of his own theories. Instead of developing some one of the manners which he has initiated, he has begun again and again with a different material or a different problem and arrived at a quite new manner. The new manner often enough contradicts some of the essential qualities of his previous work, qualities which European followers have emulated with distinction and used as the basis of further advance. In his refusal of the shackles of a fixed style he has created the illusion of infinite possible styles, like the mathematicians who have invented non-Euclidean geometries. His eternally young spirit rebels against the new style as vigorously as he rebelled against the "styles" of the nineteenth century.

Wright belongs to the international style no more than Behrens or Perret or Van de Velde. Some of these men have been ready to learn from their juniors. They have submitted in part to the disciplines of the international style. But their work is still marked by traces of the individualistic manners they achieved in their prime. Without their work the style could hardly have come into being. Yet their individualism and their relation to the past, for all its tenuousness, makes of them not so much the creators of a new style as the last representatives of Romanticism. They are more akin to the men of a hundred years ago than to the generation which has come to the fore since the War.

The continued existence of Romantic individualism is not a question of architecture alone. There is a dichotomy of the spirit more profound than any mere style can ever resolve. The case against individualism in architecture lies in the fact that Wright has been almost alone in America in achieving a distinguished architecture; while in Europe, and indeed in other parts of the world as well, an increasingly large group of architects work successfully within the disciplines of the new style.

There is a basic cleavage between the international style and the half-modern architecture of the beginning of the present century. We must not forget the debt that Le Corbusier, Gropius, Miës van der Rohe, Oud and the rest owe to the older men with whom they studied. We must not forget such exceptional monuments of the nineteenth century as the Crystal Palace. We must not dismiss as lacking historical significance the fine sense of proportion and the vigorous purity of the Classical Revival, or the splendid theories and the stupid practice of the Gothic Revival. Even the absurdities of Romantic artificial ruins and the linear and naturalistic ornament of 1900 have a place in the pedigree of the contemporary style. But the new style after ten years of existence and growth may now be studied for itself without continual reference to the immediate past.

There are certain times when a new period truly begins despite all the preparation that may be traced behind the event. Such a time came immediately after the War, when the international style came into being in France, in Holland, and in Germany. Indeed, if we follow the projects of the War years made by the Austrian Loos and the Italian Sant' Elia, it may appear that the new style was preparing on an even broader front. While the innovations of the half-moderns were individual and independent to the point of divergence, the innovations of their juniors were parallel and complementary, already informed by the coherent spirit of a style in the making.

It is particularly in the early work of three men, Walter Gropius in Germany, Oud in Holland, and Le Corbusier in France, that the various steps in the inception of the new style must be sought. These three with Mies van der Rohe in Germany remain the great leaders of modern architecture.

Gropius' factory at Alfeld, built just before the War, came nearer to an integration of the new style than any other edifice built before 1922. In industrial architecture the tradition of the styles of the past was not repressive, as many factories of the nineteenth century well illustrate. The need for using modern construction throughout and for serving function directly was peculiarly evident. Hence it was easier for Gropius to advance in this field beyond his master, Behrens, than it would have been in any other. The walls of the Alfeld factory are screens of glass with spandrels of metal at the floor levels. The crowning band of brickwork does not project beyond these screens. The purely mechanical elements are frankly handled and give interest to a design fundamentally so regular as to approach monotony. There is no applied ornamental decoration except the lettering. The organization of the parts of the complex structure is ordered by logic and consistency rather than by axial symmetry.

Yet there are traces still of the conceptions of traditional architecture. The glass screens are treated like projecting bays between the visible supports. These supports are sheathed with brick so that they appear like the last fragments of the solid masonry wall of the past. The entrance is symmetrical and heavy. For all its simplicity it is treated with a decorative emphasis. Gropius was not destined to achieve again so fine and so coherent a production in the contemporary style before the Bauhaus in 1926. There he profited from the intervening æsthetic experimentation of the Dutch Neoplasticists. The Bauhaus is something more than a mere development from the technical triumph of the Alfeld factory. (See illustrations on pages 150 ff.)

During the years of the War, Oud in Holland came into contact with the group of Dutch cubist painters led by Mondriaan and Van Doesburg, who called themselves Neoplasticists. Their positive influence on his work at first was negligible. Oud remained for a time still a disciple of Berlage, whose half-modern manner he had previously followed rather closely. He profited also by his study of the innovations of Wright, whose work was already better known in Europe than in America. Then he sought consciously to achieve a Neoplasticist architecture and, from 1917 on, the influence of Berlage and Wright began to diminish. At the same time he found in concrete an adequate material for the expression of new conceptions of form. Oud's projects were increasingly simple, vigorous and geometrical. On the analogy of abstract painting he came to realize the æsthetic potentialities of planes in three dimensions with which Wright had already experimented. He reacted sharply against the picturesqueness of the other followers of Berlage and sought with almost Greek fervor to arrive at a scheme of proportions ever purer and more regular.

In his first housing projects carried out for the city of Rotterdam in 1918 and 1919 he did not advance as far as in his unexecuted projects. But at Oud-Mathenesse in 1921–22, although he was required to build the whole village in traditional materials and to continue the use of conventional roofs, the new style promised in his projects came into being. The avoidance of picturesqueness, the severe horizontality of the composition, the perfect simplicity and consistency which he achieved in executing a very complex project, all announced the conscious creation of a body of æsthetic disciplines.

Oud-Mathenesse exceeded Gropius' Alfeld factory in significance if not in impressiveness. Gropius made his innovations primarily in technics, Oud in design. He undoubtedly owed the initial impetus to the Neoplasticists, but his personal manner had freed itself from dependence on painting. The models Van Doesburg made of houses in the early twenties, in collaboration with other Neoplasticists, with their abstract play of volumes and bright colors, had their own direct influence in Germany.

But the man who first made the world aware that a new style was being born was Le Corbusier. As late as 1916, well after his technical and sociological theorizing had begun, his conceptions of design were still strongly marked by the Classical symmetry of his master Perret. His plans, however, were even more open than those of Wright. In his housing projects of the next few years he passed rapidly beyond his master Perret and beyond Behrens and Loos, with whom he had also come in contact. His *Citrohan* house model of 1921 was the thorough expression of a conception of architecture as radical technically as Gropius' factory and as novel æsthetically as Oud's village. The enormous window area and the terraces made possible by the use of ferroconcrete, together with the asymmetry of the composition, undoubtedly produced a design more thoroughly infused with a new spirit, more completely freed from the conventions of the past than any thus far projected.

The influence of Le Corbusier was the greater, the appearance of a new style the more remarked, because of the vehement propaganda which he contributed to the magazine *L'Esprit Nouveau*, 1920–1925. Since then, moreover, he has written a series of books effectively propagandizing his technical and æsthetic theories. In this way his name has become almost synonymous with the new architecture and it has been praised or condemned very largely in his person. But he was not, as we have seen, the only innovator nor was the style as it came generally into being after 1922 peculiarly his. He crystallized; he dramatized; but he was not alone in creating.

When in 1922 he built at Vaucresson his first house in the new style, he failed to equal the purity of design and the boldness of construction of the *Citrohan* project. But the houses that immediately followed this, one for the painter Ozenfant, and another for his parents outside Vevey, passed further beyond the transitional stage than anything that Oud or Gropius were to build for several more years. Ozenfant's sort of cubism, called Purism, had perhaps inspired Le Corbusier in his search for sources of formal inspiration for a new architecture. But on the whole Le Corbusier in these early years turned for precedent rather to steamships than to painting. Some of his early houses, such as that for the sculptor Miestchaninoff at Boulogne-sur-Seine, were definitely naval in feeling. But this marine phase was soon over like Oud's strictly Neoplasticist phase, or the Expressionist period in the work of the young architects of Germany. Various external influences helped to free architecture from the last remnants of a lingering traditionalism. The new style displayed its force in the rapidity with which it transmuted them beyond recognition.

Miës van der Rohe advanced toward the new style less rapidly at first than Gropius. Before the War he had simplified, clarified, and lightened the domestic style of Behrens to a point that suggests conscious inspiration from Schinkel and Persius. After the War in two projects for skyscrapers entirely of metal and glass he carried technical innovation even further than Gropius, further indeed than anyone has yet gone in practice. These buildings would have been pure volume, glazed cages supported from within, on a scale such as not even Paxton in the nineteenth century would have dreamed possible. However, in their form, with plans based on clustered circles or sharp angles, they were extravagantly Romantic and strongly marked by the contemporary wave of Expressionism in Germany.

It was in Miës' projects of 1922 that his true significance as an æsthetic innovator first appeared. In a design for a country house he broke with the conception of the wall as a continuous plane surrounding the plan and built up his composition of sections of intersecting planes. Thus he achieved, still with the use of supporting walls, a greater openness even than Le Corbusier with his ferroconcrete skeleton construction. Miës' sense of proportions remained as serene as before the War and even more pure. This project and the constructions of Oud and Le Corbusier in this year emphasize that it is just a decade ago that the new style came into existence.

The four leaders of modern architecture are Le Corbusier, Oud, Gropius and Miës van der Rohe. But others as well as they, Rietveld in Holland, Lurçat in France, even Mendelsohn in Germany, for all his lingering dalliance with Expressionism, took parallel steps of nearly equal importance in the years just after the War. The style did not spring from a single source but came into being generally. The writing of Oud and Gropius, and to a greater degree that of Le Corbusier, with the frequent publication of their projects of these years, carried the principles of the new style abroad. These projects have indeed become more famous than many executed buildings.

From the first there were also critics, who were not architects, to serve as publicists. Everyone who was interested in the creation of a modern architecture had to come to terms with the nascent style. The principles of the style that appeared already plainly by 1922 in the projects and the executed buildings of the leaders, still control today an ever increasing group of architects throughout the world.

III

F U N C T I O N A L I S M

In part the principles of the international style were from the first voiced in the manifestoes which were the order of the day. In part they have remained unconscious, so that even now it is far simpler to sense them than to explain them or to state them categorically. Many who appear to follow them, indeed, refuse to admit their validity. Some modern critics and groups of architects both in Europe and in America deny that the æsthetic element in architecture is important, or even that it exists. All æsthetic principles of style are to them meaningless and unreal. This new conception, that building is science and not art, developed as an exaggeration of the idea of functionalism.

In its most generally accepted form the idea of functionalism is sufficiently elastic. It derives its sanctions from both Greek and Gothic architecture, for in the temple as well as in the cathedral the æsthetic expression is based on structure and function. In all the original styles of the past the æsthetic is related to, even dependent on, the technical. The supporters of both the Classical Revival and the Mediæval Revival in the nineteenth century were ready to defend much of their practice by functionalist arguments. The so-called rationalism of architects like Schinkel and Labrouste was a type of functionalism. It is vigorously advocated, moreover, in the archæological criticism of Viollet-le-Duc and the ethical criticism of Pugin and Ruskin. Morris and his disciples brought this sort of functionalist theory down to our own day.

The doctrine of the contemporary anti-æsthetic functionalists is much more stringent. Its basis is economic rather than ethical or archæological. Leading European critics, particularly Siegfried Giedion, claim with some justice that architecture has such immense practical problems to deal with in the modern world that æsthetic questions must take a secondary place in architectural criticism. Architects like Hannes Meyer go further. They claim that interest in proportions or in problems of design for their own sake is still an unfortunate remnant of nineteenth century ideology. For these men it is an absurdity to talk about the modern style in terms of æsthetics at all. If a building provides adequately, completely, and without compromise for its purpose, it is to them a good building, regardless of its appearance. Modern construction receives from them a straightforward expression; they use standardized parts whenever possible and they avoid ornament or unnecessary detail. Any elaboration of design, any unnecessary use of specially made parts, any applied decoration would add to the cost of the building. It is, however, nearly impossible to organize and execute a complicated building without making some choices not wholly determined by technics and economics. One may therefore refuse to admit that intentionally functionalist building is quite without a potential æsthetic element. Consciously or unconsciously the architect must make free choices before his design is completed. In these choices the European functionalists follow, rather than go against, the principles of the general contemporary style. Whether they admit it or not is beside the point.

In America also there are both architects and critics who consider architecture not an art, as it has been in the past, but merely a subordinate technic of industrial civilization. Æsthetic criticism of building appears to them nearly as meaningless as æsthetic criticism of road building. Their attitude has been to some extent a beneficial one in its effect on American building, even from the æsthetic point of view. Most European critics feel rightly that American engineers have always been far more successful with their technics than American architects with their æsthetics.

But to the American functionalists, unfortunately, design is a commodity like ornament. If the client insists, they still try to provide it in addition to the more tangible commodities which they believe rightly should come first. But they find one sort of design little better than another and are usually as ready to provide zigzag trimmings as rhythmical fenestration. For ornament can be added after the work is done and comes into no direct relation with the handling of function and structure. American modernism in design is usually as superficial as the revivalism which preceded it. Most American architects would regret the loss of applied ornament and imitative design. Such things serve to obscure the essential emptiness of skyscraper composition.

The European functionalists are primarily builders, and architects only unconsciously. This has its advantages even for architecture as an art. Critics should be articulate about problems of design; but architects whose training is more technical than intellectual, can afford to be unconscious of the æsthetic effects they produce. So, it may be assumed, were many of the great builders of the past. Since the works of the European functionalists usually fall within the limits of the international style, they may be claimed among its representatives. (Page 223 f.) Naturally these doctrinaires achieve works of æsthetic distinction less often than some others who practice the art of architecture as assiduously as they pursue the science of building.

The American functionalists claim to be builders first. They are surely seldom architects in the fullest sense of the word. They are ready, as the European functionalists are not, to deface their building with bad architectural design if the client demands it. Nor can they claim for their skyscrapers and apartment houses the broad sociological justification that exists for the workers' housing, the schools and hospitals of Europe. On the whole, American factories, where the client expects no money to be spent on design, are better buildings and at least negatively purer in design than those constructions in which the architect is forced by circumstances to be more than an engineer. Technical developments, moreover, are rapidly forcing almost all commercial and industrial building into the mould of the international style.

It is not necessary to accept the contentions of the functionalists that there is no new style or even to consider their own work still another kind of architecture. While the older generation has continued faithful to individualism, a set of general æsthetic principles has come into use. While the functionalists continue to deny that the æsthetic element in architecture is important, more and more buildings are produced in which these principles are wisely and effectively followed without sacrifice of functional virtues.

IV

A FIRST PRINCIPLE

Architecture as Volume

Contemporary methods of construction provide a cage or skeleton of supports. This skeleton as it appears before the building is enclosed is familiar to everyone. Whether the supports are of metal or of reinforced concrete, the effect from a distance is of a grille of verticals and horizontals. For protection against the weather it is necessary that this skeleton should be in some way enclosed by walls. In traditional masonry construction the walls were themselves the supports. Now the walls are merely subordinate elements fitted like screens between the supports or carried like a shell outside of them. Thus the building is like a boat or an umbrella with strong internal support and a continuous outside covering. In the buildings of the past, support and protection were both provided by the same masonry wall. It is true that supporting wall sections are still sometimes used in combination with skeleton construction. (Pages 133 and 217.) Isolated supports, piers of metal or reinforced concrete, are, however, normal and typical.

Plans may be worked out with far greater freedom than in the past. The piers of modern construction are so slight in section that they create no serious obstruction. If in given cases they might interfere, occasional supports may be omitted and their burden carried by cantilevering. Entire façades are frequently cantilevered and the screen walls set some distance outside the supports. (Pages 118 and 172.) Symbolically the indication of modern plans is reduced to points representing support and lines representing separation and protection from the weather. No longer do we find the solid blocks of bearing walls and piers of masonry. The plan can be composed almost entirely in terms of the needs it must provide for, with only minimal concessions to the inescapable needs of sound construction.

The effect of mass, of static solidity, hitherto the prime quality of architecture, has all but disappeared; in its place there is an effect of volume, or more accurately, of plane surfaces bounding a volume. The prime architectural symbol is no longer the dense brick but the open box. Indeed, the great majority of buildings are in reality, as well as in effect, mere planes surrounding a volume. With skeleton construction enveloped only by a protective screen, the architect can hardly avoid achieving this effect of surface of volume unless, in deference to traditional design in terms of mass, he goes out of his way to obtain the contrary effect.

The European functionalists conform unconsciously to this principle of the international style without accepting its validity as an æsthetic discipline. The American functionalists, however, often load their surfaces, thus obscuring with an effect of solidity and weight the non-supporting character of their wall screens. If they design at all—and except in factories the client usually demands some sort of applied design—they design still in mass. A striking contrast is familiar to everyone as it appears in buildings under construction: the strong light cage of steel, and the heavy solid-appearing walls with which it is gradually covered. The greater simplicity of the newer skyscrapers, the increase in the window area and the growing awareness of the international style are reducing little by little this superficial heaviness. But thus far the more expensive the building, the more surely is there a conflict between its true character as an enclosed steel cage and the apparent mass of its vertical buttressing and its pyramidal composition.

Of course this pyramidal composition is required in high buildings by the zoning laws. Present American zoning laws are at best pseudo-functional. They attempt merely to ameliorate the sociological and technical difficulties inherent in crowding tall buildings together on narrow streets. Proper zoning laws would require the spacing of skyscrapers far enough apart so that they might rise straight to the top without setbacks. Setbacks complicate the structure and provide relatively little terrace space, nor do they adequately protect the light and air of neighboring buildings. The criticism that accepts the present zoning laws as beneficent is mistaken. If that criticism is æsthetic, it rests on the false assumption that skyscrapers are mere enlargements of the masonry towers of the past. If the criticism is functional, it has failed to go to the root of the urban problem. Skyscrapers have their proper place in the modern city, but they must be so widely spaced that they relieve congestion rather than aggravate it.

The McGraw-Hill Building (Page 163) comes nearest to

achieving æsthetically the expression of the enclosed steel cage, but it is still partially distorted into the old silhouette of the massive tower. The setbacks are, of course, required by the zoning law, but they are arranged without subtlety. The unnecessary pyramidal feature which crowns the structure is inexcusably heavy. Yet the architect, Raymond Hood, in the Daily News Building of the previous year, which is in other ways less pure in expression, handled the setbacks so that they did not suggest steps and brought his building to a clear stop without decorative or terminal features. This has also been justly criticised by those functionalists whose ideology is more European. For the water-tanks and elevator machinery which have to find a place on top of a large building are there, hidden within the shell of the main structure.

These various objections, which place both of these buildings as something less than distinguished architecture, are implicit in American conditions. Only the acceptance of a thoroughgoing æsthetic discipline by our architects would make it possible for our skyscrapers to be finer than our factories. For our factories, unless the client has called for embellishment, are like the constructions of the European functionalists. They exist clearly and effectively as the surfaces of volumes, even though the architect has never accepted the æsthetic principle that they should do so.

In the past the great styles became something more than a certain sort of construction, or a certain repertory of ornament. Post and lintel construction was used in Egyptian architecture as well as Greek. Romanesque churches achieved nearly as great a science and elaboration of vaulting as did the later ones of the Gothic age. The Gothic architects emphasized the impression of height and of orderly multiplicity of organically related parts; the Greek architects so adjusted their design as to give their buildings the plastic somatic character of their sculpture. Style is character, style is expression; but even character must be displayed and expression may be conscious and clear, or muddled and deceptive. The architect who builds in the international style seeks to display the true character of his construction and to express clearly his provision for function. He prefers such an organization of his general composition, such a use of available surface materials, and such a handling of detail as will increase rather than contradict the prime effect of surface of volume. '

In giving this effect the flat roofs normal with modern methods of construction have an essential æsthetic significance. Roofs with a single slant, however, have occasionally been used with success. For they are less massive and simpler than the gabled roofs usual on the buildings of the past. Flat roofs are so much more useful that slanting or rounded roofs are only exceptionally justified.

The clarity of the impression of volume is diminished by any sort of complication. Volume is felt as immaterial and weightless, a geometrically bounded space. Subsidiary projecting parts of a building are likely to appear solid. Hence a compact and unified solution of a complex problem will be best æsthetically as well as economically. The massiveness of the architecture of the past was felt as gravitational, with surface and content one. Being heavy, massive architecture demanded the appearance of support such as could be given by a piling up of the parts. This sort of stability, like that of a wood pile, our tenuous cage construction does not give. The sense of internal support is, on the other hand, increased by the avoidance of subsidiary parts and by the achievement as far as possible of the effect of a single volume with continuous surfaces.

Thus as a corollary of the principle of surface of volume there is the further requirement that the surfaces shall be unbroken in effect, like a skin tightly stretched over the supporting skeleton.

The apparent tensions of a masonry wall are directly gravitational, although they are actually modified more or less by the use of lintels and arches. The apparent tensions of screen walls are not thus polarized in a vertical direction, but are felt to exist in all directions, as in a stretched textile. Hence the breaking of the wall surface by placing windows at the inner instead of at the outer edge of the wall is a serious fault of design. (Pages 159 and 232.) For the glass of the windows is now an integral part of the enclosing screen rather than a hole in the wall as it was in masonry construction.

Where the roof is supported on sections of wall rather than on isolated posts, only the non-supporting sections are really screens. Yet the discipline of the general style is better served if the contrast between the supporting wall surfaces and the non-supporting surfaces is not over-emphasized. Such construction with a reinforced concrete roof slab is still more like the normal modern cage construction than like traditional masonry construction. (Page 133.) This is a special case which demands on the part of the designer unusual tact and sense of the style. Such exceptions must always be borne in mind by the critic. Their successful incorporation in the style according to the spirit, if not the letter, of the fundamental disciplines makes the existence of a contemporary style difficult to dispute.

The ordering of the openings in the wall surface is quite as important as the avoidance of apparent reveals in the preservation of the integrity of the wall plane. But questions of order fall more logically in a later section of this discussion. Needless to say, the more consistently a surface is arranged, the more conspicuous will be its character as a surface. Contemporary buildings often have entire walls of transparent glass constituting one enormous window. The frames of the panes in such walls must be light enough to be distinguished from true supports. (Pages 156 and 191.) Otherwise these subordinate divisions will so break up the surface into panels that its continuous character is confused. Even though the independent supporting skeleton is perfectly clearly seen behind, such a panelled treatment appears to have weight if not mass. Such altogether transparent walls are not by any means the easiest for the architect to handle effectively. They no longer appear the extreme toward which the development of the contemporary style inevitably leads. Indeed, as the Crystal Palace of the last century and the steel and glass department stores of 1900 suggest, such maximal fenestration was a preparation for the development of a more general principle of modern design: that of emphasizing the surfaces whether they are opaque or transparent.

Windows constitute a more important element in modern architecture than they have in any architecture since that of the Gothic cathedrals. They are the most conspicuous features of modern exterior design. Their handling is therefore an æsthetic problem of the greatest importance. The very effect of volume that is sought in choosing surfacing materials can easily be diluted or contradicted by bad fenestration.

Window frames unavoidably break the general wall surface and if they are heavy tend to make the window a mere hole in the wall quite as much as do reveals. (Pages 139 and 179.) Light simple frames, preferably of durable non-corroding metal in standardized units, are to be desired as much æsthetically as practically. (Pages 155 and 173.) Non-corroding metals are still rather expensive. Moreover standardized metal frames have not yet come into use everywhere. But the general development in this direction is undeniable and one of happy augury for the contemporary style.

Wooden window frames are becoming a makeshift. Yet many architects have been able to make them appear hardly heavier than metal ones. Some of the finest examples of fenestration in modern architecture are executed in wood. (Pages 113 and 127.) Of course the elegance which is obtained by light frames and muntins goes for nothing if the windows are badly subdivided and badly placed in the general design.

The spirit of the principle of surface covers many exceptions to its letter. The type of construction represented by Miës van der Rohe's Barcelona pavilion, (Page 187), as well as that represented in Le Corbusier's house at Le Pradet, (Page 133), leads to a treatment of surfaces sensibly different from that which has been primarily stressed here. These works, nevertheless, testify that their designers are extending the possibilities of the contemporary style. In each of these buildings the surfaces are emphasized and their continuity made evident although their relation to the supporting construction is less simple than in most buildings.

In the Barcelona pavilion the walls are screens but they do not define a fixed volume. The volume beneath the post-supported slab roof is in a sense bounded by imaginary planes. The walls are independent screens set up within this total volume, having each a separate existence and creating subordinate volumes. The design is unified by the slab roof on its regular supports, not by the usual continuous exterior screen wall.

In the Le Pradet house by Le Corbusier sections of rubble masonry wall provide the main support and isolated piers are used only subordinately. These supporting sections are unbroken by windows and widely separated by wall areas entirely of glass. As in the Barcelona pavilion the enclosing volume is defined by the continuous slab roof. The exterior surfaces are not continuous because they are of two sorts, unbroken masonry walls and intervening glass screens. But the two sorts of surfaces are both treated in a way to emphasize their specific characters. The supporting walls are rough and solid in appearance; the intermediate screens, light, smooth and transparent. The two sorts are carefully related in proportion. The use of a special type of construction suited to the particular problem of a Riviera country house has led to a special type of design. The expression is related to the general principle of surface of volume but not restricted by it. Thus the prime principles of the great styles of the past were applied in exceptional cases. This special type of design has its place in the general contemporary style as much as astylar buildings in Greek architecture or unvaulted construction in the Gothic.

The principle of surface of volume intelligently understood will always lead to special applications where the construction is not the typical cage or skeleton of supports surrounded by a protecting screen. The apparent exception may not prove the validity of the general principle, but it undoubtedly indicates its elasticity. Rigid rules of design are easily broken once and for all; elastic principles of architecture grow and flourish. Forgetting neither the origins in a certain type of construction nor the possibilities which lie always ahead, architects should find in such principles as that of surface of volume a sure and continuing guidance as the international style develops.

V

S U R F A C I N G M A T E R I A L

The character of surface of volume is not expressed merely by the general design of a modern building; the actual materials of the surface itself are of the utmost importance. The ubiquitous stucco, which still serves as the hall-mark of the contemporary style, has the æsthetic advantage of forming a continuous even covering. But if the stucco is rough, the sharpness of the design, which facilitates apprehension of the building's volume, is blunted. (Page 155.) Rough stucco, because of its texture and because it recalls the stucco-covered buildings of the past, is likely to suggest mass. All stucco, rough or smooth, is subject to cracking and streaking; if painted, it is even less likely to preserve its original surface and color. Stucco, like exposed concrete, must be considered inferior to more solid sheathing except where the large scale of the construction makes the flaws that come with time relatively inconspicuous. A material like stucco but elastic and with a wide color range, which could be laid over various bases, would be ideal.

Wooden sheathing is admirable in the special case of modern construction in wood. It is not as durable as stone or brick, yet as we are aware in America, it can well outlast a century if it is kept painted. Smooth matchboarding is desirable because overlapping or stripped joints mar the surface, particularly in small-scale construction. (Page 227.) In interiors and on temporary buildings, plywood panels are excellent since they are large in area and smooth. (Page 119.) They may be painted or left to show the grain. Any enframement suggesting panelling seriously breaks the continuity of surface and should be avoided.

As in the architecture of the past, the finest materials for wall surfacing are stones, granites and marbles. (Pages 135 and 187 f.) Unless they are large in area, however, the separate units are likely to appear like the faces of blocks of masonry, suggesting weight and mass. As in Byzantine architecture it is possible to use plates so that their true character as sheathing is evident. Rich natural materials are expensive and hence more suitable in construction of a monumental or luxurious character than in ordinary buildings. Artificial plaques of various sorts and metal plates exposed or painted have similar advantages and will doubtless be increasingly used. (Pages 113 and 169.) In any sort of plate covering it is important that the plates be so joined that the surface is as little broken as possible. Graining, moreover, should be so disposed as to emphasize the continuity of the whole wall and not, as in the past, to produce symmetrical patterns. It is also important that the surface remain a plane without

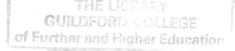

convexities and concavities. Otherwise the effect becomes picturesque and the sense of equal tension in all directions is destroyed.

Plate sheathing has the distinct advantage of similarity in texture and scale to the glass panes of the windows. The massiveness of the walls of the past was emphasized by the contrast between the wall surfaces and the windows. The walls appeared the more solid for being visibly penetrated by infrequent holes. Today the general consistency of the design and the sense of continuous surface is emphasized by reducing the contrast between the transparent and the opaque sections of the bounding walls. Windows should be independent in character but not a breach in the general coherence of the surface.

Burned clay products are more frequently used than plate sheathing. Brick is from the practical point of view the most satisfactory inexpensive surfacing material in general use. It may be equally well used for screen walls and for sections of supporting wall where they supplement skeleton construction. Yet from an æsthetic point of view, brick is undoubtedly less satisfactory than other materials, including stucco. Indeed, brick is often covered with stucco even by architects who claim to be uninfluenced by æsthetic considerations. (Page 219.) This concession to the principle of achieving a smooth continuous surface is an important instance of the exaggeration of the functionalists' anti-æsthetic claims.

Brick, when laid conventionally, suggests a solid supporting wall even where that does not exist. Even a screen wall of brick appears to retain something of the mass and the dead weight of the architecture of the past. The use of brick tends to give a picturesqueness which is at variance with the fundamental character of the modern style. Bricks are more or less rough in texture, often irregular in color, and quite unrelated in scale to the panes of the windows. (Page 217.)

Nevertheless, much can be done to emphasize continuity of surface. If the color of the mortar be near that of the brick, and the bricks relatively even in value and texture, the bonding pattern need not be strikingly evident. The actual material of a wall surface of considerable area is then relatively inconspicuous. (Pages 167 and 183.) On the whole, the cheapest, the most common types of brick and the most straightforward method of laying have fortunately proved best. Since brick is permanent in color and not subject to cracking and streaking, it is in the long run actually superior æsthetically to stucco for large-scale constructions. (Pages 189 and 151.)

A different shape of brick and a different method of laying might be developed which would be more satisfactory æsthetically as well as practically than present types and methods. Increase in size would be only a disadvantage since it would make the individual unit more conspicuous. Indeed, the finest surfaces from the point of view of the contemporary style are those attained in eighteenth century Holland with very small smooth bricks and thin joints.

Ordinary terra cotta blocks or concrete blocks of the cheapest sort are less satisfactory in appearance and more suggestive of traditional masonry than even the commonest brickwork. Concrete slabs even though they may attain the scale of plate sheathing are also too irregular in texture and variable in color to be acceptable except at the economic minimum.

In the range of constructions of medium cost and medium size glazed tile laid with continuous vertical as well as horizontal joints provides a material that vies in æsthetic effectiveness with plate sheathing. (Page 175.) The shape of the units may be such that all suggestion of the traditional masonry block is lost. The texture is smooth and permanent; the color possibilities are wide. The small scale of the individual tiles is less harmonious with the panes of the windows than are large plaques, but the individual tiles are less independently assertive. An adjustment of the minor rhythm of the individual tiles to the rhythm of the windows and the structural elements is a possible refinement. Tiles properly laid give even more surely than bricks a continuous surface pattern like the texture of a fabric. They also quite avoid the suggestion of a supporting masonry wall. Their pattern is more regular than the graining of natural materials used in sheathing plates. Marble or granite plates are certainly richer; tile, however, fulfills better the rigid letter of the principle of surface.

Glass bricks and translucent glass plates are types of surfacing materials which may occasionally take the place of true windows. (Pages 172 and 193.) In certain buildings various panes of transparent, translucent, and opaque glass have been combined together for entire walls. The effect is rich and harmonious but perhaps too fragile for permanent architecture. Glass bricks provide a means of carrying light through the wall without a window frame. When they are of the same or related scale they combine best æsthetically with other unitary coverings such as brick and tile. (Page 147.)

In the choice of surfacing materials the architect is far from free. Factories will hardly have marble sheathing; yet because they have very large wall areas, the surfacing material itself is less noticeable. Brick appears the best material for large and inexpensive construction, tile in the middle range and plate sheathing for exceptional buildings. In the last the architect has the opportunity to seek to the full the possibilities of richness and individual distinction which the contemporary style affords quite as much as the styles of the past.

VI

A SECOND PRINCIPLE

Concerning Regularity

T he patterns of Gothic fenestration were ordered according to definite conceptions of design derived from structure and leading more and more to arbitrary decoration. Today the patterns of windows, the composition of the parts of contemporary architecture, must also be ordered according to an æsthetic principle if a contemporary style exist. The functionalists claim that they order their designs according to practical considerations alone. Yet even they, because of the economic force of standardization, accept a discipline of design not dissimilar to that found in the work of contemporary architects who grant the importance of æsthetic considerations. Beside the principle of surface of volume already discussed there is a second controlling principle, evident in the productions of the international style including the work of the European functionalists.

This second principle of contemporary style in architecture has to do with regularity. The supports in skeleton construction are normally and typically spaced at equal distances in order that strains may be equalized. (Pages 117 and 149.) Thus most buildings have an underlying regular rhythm which is clearly seen before the outside surfaces are applied. Moreover, economic considerations favor the use of standardized parts throughout. Good modern architecture expresses in its design this characteristic orderliness of structure and this similarity of parts by an æsthetic ordering which emphasizes the underlying regularity. Bad modern design contradicts this regularity. Regularity is, however, relative and not absolute in architecture.

The varied purposes which most buildings serve cannot be completely regularized. A loft building in a city may be, and often is, regular throughout except for the entrances and the elevators. (Page 162.) The many purposes which each floor serves are so nearly alike that the same plan and elevation may be used throughout. Few buildings, however, are so simple. In most cases, within a structure as regular as possible and using similar parts the architect must provide for many varying functions related in various different ways to one another. In a hotel, for example, although the suites considered as units repeat themselves, the lobbies, dining rooms and kitchens serve the whole building and are on an entirely different scale. Within an individual dwelling house it is obvious that there are relatively fewer interchangeable elements. The functional requirements of the different rooms are even more varied. The bathroom, for example, makes far more elaborate specific demands than the living room, but it is possible to take care of them in much less space.

Thus technically the prime architectural problem of distribution is to adjust the irregular and unequal demands of function to regular construction and the use of standardized parts.

Just as the æsthetic principle of surface of volume has been derived from the fact that architecture no longer has solid supporting walls, the second principle, that of regularity, depends on the regularity typical of the underlying skeleton of modern construction. This second principle is expressed in an ordering of design more consistent than would result merely from the æsthetically unconscious use of regular structure and standardized parts for varying and complicated functions. Thus the expression receives a visible regularity and consistency. This is the symbol of the underlying technics, which in the completed building are known rather than seen. (Pages 149 and 161.)

It must be remembered that the nearer approaches to absolute regularity are also approaches to monotony, as the earlier reference to the loft building will have suggested. The principle of regularity refers to a means of organization, a way of giving definite form to an architectural design, rather than to an end which is sought for itself. As an end, regularity is modified by the equal necessity, understood in all æsthetic organization, of achieving a proper degree of interest. What constitutes a proper degree of interest is hardly to be determined in theory.

Many critics, more familiar with the architecture of the past than with that of the present, claim that the international style seldom if ever achieves a proper degree of interest. They miss the interest arising from the normally irregular construction of much of the architecture of the past. They fail to comprehend the new and possibly more subtle sorts of interest which derive from the principle of surface of volume or which lie in the positive application of the principle of regularity itself. The same critics, preferring the picturesqueness of less rigorous styles, are equally likely to find an insufficient amount of interest in Greek architecture and in the work of those architects who attempted to revive the Greek style a hundred years ago. It is undoubtedly true that much minor architecture of the Greek Revival was monotonous and it is equally true of much of the building in the contemporary style. Even this monotony, arising from the too rigid application of the principle of regularity may, however, be preferred to the confused vagaries of the intervening period, when the principle of regularity was largely abjured. Within the field of a given style, however, what constitutes a proper degree of interest is in practice sufficiently clear: the Parthenon would not be improved by being as complicated as the Propylæa or the Erechtheum. The great modern architects have known how to achieve interest in their compositions while exercising a truly classic restraint.

In the various styles of the past a principle of axial symmetry controlled design rather than a principle of regularity as that is understood here. The Greek meaning of symmetry, "a due proportion of the several parts," was nearly equivalent to this special meaning of regularity. But Greek symmetry was usually bilateral as well as regular. Axial symmetry has generally been used to achieve the ordering of irregularity, as in Baroque architecture, dominating and relating the confusion of independent features and elaborate detail. Modern standardization gives automatically a high degree of consistency in the parts. Hence modern architects have no need of the discipline of bilateral or axial symmetry to achieve æsthetic order. Asymmetrical schemes of design are actually preferable æsthetically as well as technically. For asymmetry certainly heightens the general interest of the composition. (Pages 175 and 207.) Function in most types of contemporary building is more directly expressed in asymmetrical form.

Sometimes asymmetry will be strong and positive, marked by

emphasis on a real axis well off the center. (Page 151.) In other cases the general effect may suggest symmetry, but there will be no stronger emphasis at the center than at some other point. (Page 141.) But in any case the avoidance of symmetry should not be arbitrary or distorted.

The mark of the bad modern architect is the positive cultivation of asymmetry for decorative reasons. For that can only be done in the majority of cases at the expense of common consistency and common sense. The mark of the good modern architect, on the other hand, is that the regularity of his designs approaches bilateral symmetry. (Page 127.) Occasionally, indeed, he even reaches it. (Pages 200 and 215.) Bilateral or axial symmetry is, however, more usually the mark of the architect newly converted to the contemporary style. Such men tend to retain it as an irrevocable traditional discipline, failing to apprehend the full implication of the new discipline of regularity which has replaced it.

Structure today is usually highly regular for economic reasons which either did not apply to masonry structure or were given less emphasis in the architecture of the past. Most functions are not regular in the sense of being similar to one another. Hence the natural expression of the various functions grouped in one building is not symmetrical. The difficulties inherent in fitting the various functions of the modern dwelling house into an eighteenth century shell, which is both relatively regular and rigidly symmetrical, make this clearly evident. The international style does not attempt to force irregular functions into a symmetrical shell. It does aim to adjust rationally the provision for irregular functions to regular structure and to express this adjustment in a clear and consistent design. Fortunately, economic considerations offer the advantage to regularity over irregularity in the arrangement of the parts and in detail quite as much as in the general structure. (Pages 163 and 183.) The functionalists often seem to follow here exactly the same principle of regularity as those who are conscious of a formal æsthetic discipline. (Page 219.)

Complete provision for function might seem to demand, for example, that each function receive unique treatment: that every window be of different shape and size, placed without formal geometrical relation to the others. Working on the principle of regularity, the ingenious architect is able to provide for all the varied functions which windows serve by means of windows of the same size, or at least built up of related units. (Page 212.) In placing them he achieves a pattern, adapted to the regularity of the underlying structure, which is both ordered and expressive. Only seldom can this pattern be absolutely regular without interfering with the provision for function. But always it may be relatively regular and composed according to a definite scheme.

Analogous to, but separate from, the hidden structural skeleton, a scheme of proportions integrates and informs a thoroughly designed modern building. A geometrical web of imaginary lines on plan and in elevation composes the diverse parts and harmonizes the various elements into a single whole. (Pages 125 and 133.) Proportions, which according to the theories of the extreme functionalists are but a relic of the nineteenth century, are still the æsthetic touchstone of the best modern design.

It is in the field of proportions and in the applications of the principle of regularity that modern architects differ most from one another. Some strive to arrange all the elements of their design within a single bounding shape, thus emphasizing to the utmost the unity of volume of the given building. (Page 127.) Others prefer a more extended articulation with more emphasis on the organic relation between the parts. (Page 149.) Architects differ greatly also in their handling of those parts of a building where, as in a wind shelter on a roof, the needs of function are very easily satisfied. Often such features are entirely unconnected with the general structure of the building and have only themselves to support. The principle of regularity does not lead to an exact solution of such a problem in adjusting function to structure, since both are too readily adaptable. For the architect who seeks only to follow the rules, or for the functionalist who has no positive interest in æsthetic creation, it is safest to do that which will be least startling. But for the great architect there is the opportunity for personal lyric expression.

At times, indeed, for the architect who is quite sure of himself and who is instinctively permeated with the spirit of the æsthetic disciplines of the contemporary style, this individual lyricism may go further. It may modify, as a positive force, the restricting discipline of regularity, composing and adjusting the necessities of function and structure without breaking with the spirit of the principle. It is the condition of the existence of a true style, the price of an architecture generally high in level, that æsthetic disciplines should be rigid, but it is the privilege of genius to interpret these disciplines, even here and there to discard them altogether. The functionalists cannot admit such a conception. Their disciplines are not in intention æsthetic and they protest most vehemently against just this sort of lyricism and personal expression. Up to a certain point they are right. Sound buildings of dull design are better than monuments of architecture whose apparent brilliance of design is paid for by inadequate provision for function and by distortion of structure. But if architecture is still to be an art, great architects must be free to go forth upon new paths of design.

It is in relation to regularity that architects are exploring the elasticity of the current disciplines. The critic may not determine in advance how far, or even in what direction, the creative interpretation of the architect may go. He may, however, judge of the results and distinguish after the fact what liberties have been those of real and what of spurious genius. He can also determine what breaches of the principle of regularity are merely irrational and careless faults. The work of some architects merely fails to achieve common consistency. The work of the best functionalists is never thus slipshod; but it seldom passes beyond the attainment of common consistency. The great architects, who still consciously practice architecture as an art, add a more interesting and usually a more personal expression to the simplification and unity of design, which even the functionalists achieve.

This development of the æsthetic possibilities of the contemporary style is well illustrated in the use of oblique and rounded forms in plan and elevation. (Pages 174 and 199 ff.) Such exceptions to general rectangularity are only occasionally demanded by function and they may introduce complications in the regular skeleton of the structure. They are, of course, a definite breach of rigid regularity. Yet sometimes as in stair wells and water-tanks, function is not best served by rectangular shapes. Curved and oblique interior partitions, moreover, often make possible the more complete adjustment of available space to function, without interfering with the regular spacing of the isolated supports. (Pages 124 and 190.)

Non-rectangular shapes, particularly if they occur infrequently, introduce an æsthetic element of the highest positive interest. To them the architect of courage turns from time to time, realizing that he must employ them chiefly with the sanctions of genius and in definite opposition to the discipline of regularity. They need seldom occur in ordinary building, but in monuments where the architect feels justified in seeking for a strongly personal expression, curves will be among the elements which give most surely extreme positive or negative æsthetic value. Curved and oblique forms seldom find a place in the cheapest solution of a given problem. But if they can be afforded, they succeed, as they fail, on æsthetic grounds alone.

The functionalists, and those who are too timid to break with rigid regularity, fall rather into the æsthetic danger of repeating the commonplaces of the style. Ranges of equal-sized windows, set in an unbroken pattern, façades where ribbon of glass alternates with ribbon of stucco, broken only by an occasional stair window, are already frequent enough in Europe to have lost the interest of mere novelty. The most determined defender of the international style must admit that the too rigid application of the principle of regularity, the unimaginative repetition of the most obvious schemes of composition, has produced much very dull building. But such work is nevertheless preferable to the building of the careless modern architects who have failed even to apprehend the existence of a principle of regularity. Those who try to follow the new style without understanding it produce work which is not only dull but irritating. They abuse corner windows; they fail to avoid the visibly gabled roof; they pile up blocks as if they were still dealing with the massive architecture of the past. In designing façades they dispose the elements with an obvious and gratuitous asymmetry and they arrange their fenestration according to no discoverable principle of order, æsthetic or technical. For them the new style that they parody is merely the architecture of the half-moderns with the decoration omitted, a makeshift product of apologetic individualism.

The American functionalists are of this order although they are less given to parodying the surface of the new style. Where they do not hide their dullness under cheap cosmetics in deference to the æsthetic desires of the client, they prefer rather to group their windows in vertical bands. This gives a traditional buttress effect quite without relation to modern methods of steel cage construction. The resultant verticality of design is still admired in America, chiefly because it recalls the aspiring quality of the Gothic towers of the past. Even in buildings with predominantly horizontal window arrangement, groups of buttresses in the center or at the corners of the building are added as a concession to the client. For horizontality, which is the most conspicuous characteristic of the international style as judged in terms of effect, is still unacceptable æsthetically to the average American client.

Yet its logic is unescapable. Storeyed construction naturally produces horizontality. Most functions, moreover, require extended development in the horizontal plane—in plan, that is, rather than in elevation. Rooms are usually broader than they are high, and are most evenly illuminated by windows of the same proportion. Structural and functional horizontality is naturally expressed in façade design by architects who seek to obtain consistency to the principle of regularity. It appears quite as clearly in the work of the European functionalists who apply no æsthetic criteria, for it is the obvious and the most straightforward result of striving to provide for function with the means of modern construction. (Page 219.)

The verticality of the skyscrapers of the American functionalists is obtained by reducing the window area and increasing the weight of the screen wall. It also contradicts the storeyed character of the construction and destroys the human scale of the design. In the early evening, when the lights come on, the solid towerlike quality of the skyscraper disappears. Then, at least, it is seen as one volume divided up into horizontal storeys. Only on rear elevations, or on façades where the architect has been severely restricted by economy, is the underlying horizontality of the American commercial building visible in the daytime.

This artificial impression of solidity, this applied verticality, undoubtedly increases the visual congestion of the modern city.

The continual appeal of vertical lines tires the eyes. Even the most commercial buildings of the nineteenth century provided the reposing horizontal of an approximately even cornice line. The verticality of the skyscraper is meaningless and anarchical. Yet because the skyscraper is an American development and the international style has developed in Europe, some nationalist critics would protect our functionalist architects from the invasion of a horizontal æsthetic. If our builders might be engineers only, protected from all æsthetics, the skyscraper would necessarily be horizontal in design. For its verticality is merely an imitative garment of pseudo-style.

Horizontality is not in itself, however, a principle of the international style. Where function demands a vertical element, that also receives expression. (Pages 159 and 237.) The principle of regularity tends to increase the effect of general horizontality at the expense of the vertical elements which play but a subordinate part in most buildings. It is only the weak and imitative architect who seeks horizontality for its own sake. One of the chief vices of contemporary architecture, which has superseded in Europe the emulation of the verticality of the American skyscraper, is what may be called "fake banding," a purely decorative scheme of tying windows together in a horizontal row. Exceptionally, where the distance between separate windows is very slight, the space between may be treated as an exposed pier by rounding it or sheathing it with the material of the window frame. (Pages 163 and 207.) But ordinarily what is not window is wall and should receive the same treatment as the rest of the wall of which it is a part. (Pages 161 and 185.)

Only great artists are capable of achieving brilliant effects with the limited means. Architects are no exception. But it is the privilege of great architects to interpret the æsthetic discipline of the style according to the spirit rather than the letter. Anyone who follows the rules, who accepts the implications of an architecture that is not mass but volume, and who conforms to the principle of regularity can produce buildings which are at least æsthetically sound. (Page 167.) If these principles seem more negative than positive, it is because architecture has suffered chiefly in the last century and a half from the extension of the sanctions of genius to all who have called themselves architects.

It were better that the world build only according to the rigid anti-æsthetic theories of the extreme European functionalists than that nineteenth century debauchery of design should continue. The individualists of the early twentieth century reacted against that debauchery with its extravagance of applied ornament. But their reaction created no fixed standards. They were neither consistent in their aims nor critical enough of the results. The ornament of the half-moderns has failed to stand the test of time even as well as that of the more cultured revivalists. The continuance of this superficially novel decoration which the half-moderns originated most effectually distinguishes the mass of American modern architecture from that of Europe.

VII

A THIRD PRINCIPLE

The Avoidance of Applied Decoration

Absence of ornament serves as much as regular horizontality to differentiate superficially the current style from the styles of the past and from the various manners of the last century and a half. Applied ornament may not have been significant or important in the architecture of the past, but it certainly existed. It is easier to defend the claim that the finest buildings built since 1800 were those least ornamented. The failure of revivalism probably lay quite as much in the inability to recreate the conditions of craftmanship which once made applied ornament æsthetically valid, as in the impossibility of adapting the spirit of old styles to new methods of construction.

It would be ridiculous to state categorically that there will never be successful applied ornament in architecture again. It is nevertheless clear that conditions are today even less propitious for the production of ornament than they were during the last century. Since the middle of the eighteenth century the quality of the execution of ornament has steadily declined. Even the renaissance of craftsmanship sponsored by the Mediævalists failed to turn the tide. On the whole each generation of traditionalists has been worse served in this respect than its predecessor.

Architecture, however, has never been without other elements of decoration. For decoration may be considered to include not only applied ornament, but all the incidental features of design which give interest and variety to the whole. Architectural detail, which is required as much by modern structure as by the structure of the past, provides the decoration of contemporary architecture. Indeed, detail actually required by structure or symbolic of the underlying structure provided most of the decoration of the purer styles of the past.

The fact that there is so little detail today increases the decorative effect of what there is. Its ordering is one of the chief means by which consistency is achieved in the parts of a design. As has already been suggested in discussing window frames, the quality of the detail has very considerable importance in supporting the effect of surface of volume. It is not in contemporary architecture alone that the details of fenestration are thus important. In any simple architecture where the windows are conspicuous these decorative elements are vital to the total effect. It is easy to recall innumerable buildings of the seventeenth and eighteenth centuries of which the scale and harmony of the design has been destroyed by the introduction of large panes of glass and thin muntins at some later date. One of the surest signs of the real existence of a style of architecture is the creation of a fixed type of window detail.

The development of simple forms of standardized detail suitable to mechanical production is thus an æsthetic as well as an economic desideratum. The absence of contemporary style in inexpensive American house building is as much due to the standardization of modern window frames after eighteenth century models as to any more positive vices of design. The comparative excellence of American factory building is largely that of its metal sashes.

Important as windows have come to be in contemporary design, there are other elements of architectural detail besides. Many of these elements do not, like windows, lend themselves to complete standardization. Of these the capping of walls is of major importance. Those who employ roof projections in normal construction indicate a definite lack of feeling for contemporary style; such relics of the cornice are required only in exceptional cases. Where such projections constitute merely an unnecessary complication of the wall surface their effect is positively bad. (Page 155.) On the other hand, where more of the roof plane is visible than merely the band projecting beyond the wall, as in various types of pavilion construction, there is no such objection. Instead, the roof plane exists, like the ceiling of an interior, as the bounding surface of a volume. (Pages 187 f. and 238.) Such capping as ordinary walls require for protection against the weather is best made as inconspicuous as possible and patently no more than a seal to the wall itself. (Pages 207 and 227.)

The handling of isolated supports like the handling of wall capping is incidental rather than fundamental. The best architects, however, have shown in this a finesse equal to that of the Greek and Gothic builders. Where isolated supports pass up into a closed construction most architects indicate the coherence of the posts with the skeleton of the construction above and not with its covering surfaces. (Pages 123 and 169.) In ferroconcrete construction rounded forms are æsthetically, and usually technically, superior since they remain visually quite separate from the wall surface. The rounded form in interiors interferes less with vision and circulation than a square or oblong pier. Where fire laws do not require more complete insulation, the actual metal pier is exceedingly light and elegant. (Page 194.) In this way significance and independence can be given again to visible supports. This they had in the great styles of the past and lost only when they came to serve as a sort of applied ornament. In some cases columns may require something corresponding to the capitals of the past. In most types of construction such bracing will disappear in the supported slab. (Page 188.) In any case such subsidiary detail should follow as directly as possible the actual stresses of the construction, avoiding the symmetrical cushion shape of traditional capitals. (Page 107.)

Parapets and railings have an importance in contemporary architecture as great as that of balustrades in the architecture of the seventeenth and eighteenth centuries. In many cases the parapet is properly treated as a continuation of the wall surface, since it encloses the roof terrace just as the wall encloses the interior room space below. (Page 141.) Where open railings are used, it is important that they should be in scale not merely with the terrace they enclose, but with the structure as a whole. Moreover, the relation of the uprights and the horizontals, forming like the muntins of the windows a grille pattern, requires careful handling. A careful adjustment of the open patterned surface to the solid unpatterned surface of the walls is a mark of distinguished design. (Pages 128 and 145.)

The best architects give particular thought to matters of detail.

Although they are incidentals, they require more than incidental attention. Fine details decorate a modern design just as did the functional columns and mouldings of Greek and Gothic architecture. If there truly be a contemporary style of architecture, it must control these as well as larger matters. Careless architects leave details to chance, thus marring creditable work. Those who claim that architecture is merely science are usually conscientious enough technologists to handle with competence, if not with brilliance, such matters of detail.

Besides architectural detail, related subordinate works of sculpture and painting have on occasion been successfully used to decorate contemporary buildings without degenerating into mere applied ornament. Mural painting should not break the wall surface unnecessarily. Yet it should remain an independent entity without the addition of borders or panelling to fuse it with the architecture. Baumeister and Ozenfant, among others, have done work of this order. But there is no reason why painting less abstract should not find its place quite as satisfactorily on the walls of contemporary buildings. It is most important that mural painting should be intrinsically excellent; otherwise a plain wall is better. It need not be related, except in scale and shape, to the wall on which it is placed. Contemporary architecture cannot expect to dictate the evolution of contemporary painting, but it offers fields more considerable than the framed canvas panel.

Sculpture also ought not to be combined or merged with architecture. It should retain its own character quite separate from that of its background. This was true of the best Greek sculpture and often of that of other periods. It is particularly important today that sculpture should be isolated; for if it is actually applied, its suggestion of solid mass is carried over to the wall surface it decorates. Thus far contemporary architecture has served rather as an admirable background for wholly separate units of painting and sculpture not designed for their specific location. (Page 188.) But there is an opportunity here for collaboration which may well in the future lead to brilliant results.

Whether from these two different forms of decoration—architectural detail and related works of painting and sculpture—the contemporary style will in time develop an ornament of its own as did the styles of the past, no one can say. The supposedly novel ornament from which architecture is now freeing itself has put us on our guard against innovations which are merely decorative. The force of all self-conscious theory tends to deny the necessity for ornament as such. Some critics would even explain all the ornament on the fine architecture of the past as but an extension of free sculpture or as a continuance of inherited detail which originally had structural meaning.

Lettering is the nearest approach to arbitrary ornament used by the architects of the international style. It has, of course, a real functional purpose in advertising and in indicating the use of different parts of a large building. Clear unseriffed letter forms are most legible at a good scale and conform most harmoniously to the geometrical character of contemporary design. Letters set forward from the wall surface or in silhouette above a roof decorate a building without breaking up the wall surfaces. (Pages 119 and 215.)

In the choice of letter forms, in the spacing of letters and words, in the use of color and lighting and handsome materials, and above all in the relation of the scale of the inscription to the scale of the building there are immense possibilities for subtlety. The principle of regularity must be respected. In architectural lettering, as in printing, legibility is a prime consideration. Script forms and fantastic placing may be justified for their effectiveness in advertising, but they are on the whole unarchitectural and best avoided. (Page 173.) Like other sorts of decoration in contemporary architecture, lettering can easily be abused.

The current style sets a high but not impossible standard for decoration: better none at all unless it be good. The principle is aristocratic rather than puritanical. It aims as much at making monstrosities impossible, at which the nineteenth century so signally failed, as at assuring masterpieces, at which the nineteenth century had no very extraordinary success.

Also in the use of color the general rule is restraint. In the earliest days of the contemporary style white stucco was ubiquitous. Little thought was given to color at a time when architects were preoccupied with more essential matters. Then followed a period when the use of color began to receive considerable attention. In Holland and Germany small areas of bright elementary colors were used; in France, large areas of more neutral color. The two practices were in large part due to the influence of two different schools of abstract painting, as represented on the one hand by Mondriaan and on the other by Ozenfant. In both cases colors were artificially applied and the majority of wall surfaces remained white. (Page 123.)

At present applied color is used less. The color of natural surfacing materials and the natural metal color of detail is definitely preferred. (Page 137.) Where the metal is painted, a dark neutral tone minimizes the apparent weight of the window frame (Pages 171 and 175.) In surfaces of stucco, white or off-white, even where it is obtained with paint, is felt to constitute the natural color. The earlier use of bright color had value in attracting attention to the new style, but it could not long remain pleasing. It ceased to startle and began to bore; its mechanical sharpness and freshness became rapidly tawdry. If architecture is not to resemble billboards, color should be both technically and psychologically permanent.

Patently artificial color, moreover, makes too sharp a contrast with natural surroundings. Light and neutral tones not unduly conflicting with those of nature are more satisfactory (Page 139.) In cities, however, small areas of brilliant color may be effectively contrasted with large areas of more or neutral color. (Page 175.)

In the use of different colors on different walls much ingenuity has been expended. Structure, function and regularity provide little excuse in principle for this use of color. It is perhaps better avoided, although it has occasionally been the means of eminent success. It emphasizes strongly the effect of surface, but it breaks up the unity of volume. This way of painting interior walls to aid reflection and light distribution has been particularly abused. The use of natural materials and of such contrasts between different walls as structure and function easily provide is more satisfactory. There is no better decoration for a room than a wall of book-filled shelves. (Page 195.)

Trees and vines are a further decoration for modern architecture. Natural surroundings are at once a contrast and a background emphasizing the artificial values created by architects. Choice of site, and the arrangement of buildings upon the site: these are the prime problems of the international style in relation to natural surroundings. As far as possible the original beauties of the site should be preserved. Mere open spaces are not enough for repose; something of the ease and grace of untouched nature is needed as well.

Terraces may extend the house outside its own boundaries, but beyond the terraces the reign of nature should clearly begin. The elaborate formal garden has no place in connection with the international style. An æsthetic of right angles derived from architecture cannot be generally applied to landscape design without diminishing the reposeful contrast of the natural background. Additional planting needed for protection or shelter, however, should usually keep to straight lines and avoid the imitation of natural irregularity. Roads and paths should be laid out for efficient communication, not with picturesque curves. The function of grounds for games and of plots for vegetables and flowers usually requires a simple geometric plan.

Furthermore, small gardens in cities, or directly attached to individual houses, may often be treated as part of the architecture. (Pages 135 and 189.) Pergolas and protective walls or hedges transform these gardens into outdoor living rooms. Of such outdoor living rooms, roof terraces are the most conspicuous examples. (Pages 123 and 128.)

VIII

ARCHITECTURE AND BUILDING

T hus far in this discussion architecture has been considered as inclusive of all forms of building. Although there is no sharp break between what is in the fullest sense architecture and what is not, there is a broad differentiation between *architecture* and *building*. There exists a range, or hierarchy, of æsthetic significance. The degree to which an edifice represents consciously or unconsciously the result of an æsthetic, as well as of a technical, effort of creation determines its place in the hierarchy. The wider the opportunity for the architect within the limitations of structure and function to make judgments determined by his taste and not merely by economics, the more fully architectural will be the resultant construction. There is no rigid classification, *building*, quite devoid of the possibility of æsthetic organization. Yet buildings built at minimal cost with practical considerations dominant throughout may be held to be less fully architectural than those on which the architect has more freedom of choice in the use of materials and the distribution of the parts.

Under whatever conditions buildings are built, they tend to be more architectural as they serve more complicated functions. The more specialized the combination of functions served by a building, the more opportunity there is for the architect to achieve a design controlled by æsthetic as well as practical considerations. The more simple and repetitious the functions of a building and the more it resembles in purpose other buildings, the less likely is the architect to reach a solution of his problems formed by his own taste. American factories admirably illustrate how *building* is becoming more and more impersonal and scientific. The best European factories illustrate, however, that in the field of industrial construction there are real architectural possibilities. (Pages 117, 167 and 183.) A large house offers relatively more possibilities of architectural development, but even a loft building can be made *architecture.*

Building quite devoid of architectural character would be æsthetically neutral no matter how good it was merely as a building. Yet at the present time the majority of building is so bad technically, so much worse than neutral æsthetically, that any good building appears to have positive æsthetic value. So bad in every way have been the façades of most American commercial edifices that their rear elevations, which are at best merely sound building, seem by contrast to possess architectural quality. For in contrast to the general low level of building, the European functionalists usually reach the level of architecture, despite their refusal to aim consciously at achieving æsthetic value. Unless one is very optimistic, it seems probable that the general level of building will always be low, that bad building will always predominate. Building that is merely good, then, may be expected to continue in effect to be better than neutral æsthetically. On the whole, whether one examine contemporary architecture in terms of the international style or not, the creation of a standard of good building has been an unmixed gain. This has been due as much to the functionalists as to those who still believe in the possibility of architecture as an art. The nineteenth century produced a great deal of bad architecture and very little good building, as the functionalists delight in pointing out.

But we still have architecture: that is, edifices consciously raised above the level of mere building. Architecture is seldom merely neutral æsthetically. It is good architecture or it is bad. When it is bad, the extreme contentions of the functionalists seem justified. But when it is good, such negative contentions appear an essential denial of the important spiritual function which all art serves. Good modern architecture may be as richly and coherently imbued with the style of our day as were the great edifices of the past with that of theirs.

The functionalists, approaching architecture from the materialistic point of view of sociology, go behind the problems that are offered to the architect and refuse their sanction to those which demand a fully architectural solution. In their estimation the modern world has neither the time nor the money required to raise building to the level of architecture. Although they are usually ready to recognize and distinguish the æsthetically good and the æsthetically bad, they deny that such a distinction has significance at a time when the world has such positive need merely of good building. The question passes outside the field of architecture into the field of politics and economics. The arguments of the functionalists are not based on the actual situation in the contemporary world outside Russia. Whether they ought to or not, many clients can still afford architecture in addition to building.

A millennium of good building is as far away as any other, and it is a worthy aspiration to lay plans for it. In such a millennium, moreover, there should still be a place for architecture. Good architecture demands intelligence and taste more than money. Today architecture and building remain closely related, shading subtly one into the other. Whether or not the contemporary style should produce architecture as well as building, it certainly does so. Indeed many developments in structure and in articulation of function now incorporated in minimal building were first evolved in expensive constructions. All the leading modern architects of the international style have been technical as well as æsthetic innovators. The European functionalists who now disown Le Corbusier, and Oud, and Gropius and Miës van der Rohe first learned the science of building from them. Most American functionalists have much to learn from the leaders of the international style, even if they cannot accept sincerely the æsthetic discipline those leaders have brought into being.

On the other hand, this æsthetic discipline was derived in considerable part from an appreciative study of industrial building. It is in the plain building of the nineteenth century rather than in its elaborate architecture that the principles of the international style were foreshadowed. The most significant work of Gropius and Oud, among the leaders of modern architecture, has been in the field of inexpensive building, which they have raised to the level of real architecture.

The idea of permanence has always been associated with architecture. Many problems of building are best solved temporarily. But temporary constructions are seldom as architectural in character as those built to endure. The international style is so dependent on new methods of construction that it might seem that its principles could only apply to the most advanced known construction. Functionalists, indeed, often deny that building can be sound unless it is radical in its technics. Arguments of economics and questions of durability are often disregarded or disputed when critics discuss the continued use of wood or masonry.

In many regions wood, for example, is economically the most satisfactory material. For certain types of building its relative impermanence is not a disadvantage. Nor is there anything in wooden construction which makes it unsuitable to the æsthetic or the functional disciplines of the contemporary style. Wooden construction, as much as construction in steel or ferroconcrete, is a cage with a protective sheathing rather than a supporting wall. Thus the principle of architectural expression as surface of volume applies to it. Indeed, wood lends itself particularly well to the production of fine surfaces. Wooden construction is, also, normally regular. The principle of avoidance of ornament holds regardless of materials. (Pages 119 and 225.)

Wood does not permit all the technical audacities of steel and concrete, but within a certain range it is unusually elastic and responsive. In the past wooden construction was often called upon to imitate styles developed in masonry. Yet many half-timber houses with their great ranges of windows are surprisingly modern in conception. Today the skeleton is no longer exposed. The lighter framing used today is better protected by a continuous outside covering such as has always been used in America. (Page 227.)

The steeply slanting roofs of the Middle Ages were already replaced in the nineteenth century by roofs with an inconspicuous slant on many wooden houses. Today the heavy pyramidal effect that tall roofs produce can be successfully avoided. The weightlessness and the consistency of modern design need no longer be contradicted by so definitely traditional a feature. Skilful architects, both in Europe and America, have even succeeded in using roofs of a single slant which avoid the traditional gable and give no impression of mass. Others have used terrace roofs just as they would on houses of steel and concrete.

Wood is admirable for building in certain special conditions but it is hardly suitable in others where the fire hazard is great, or for monumental architecture. If, however, wooden construction is to be controlled by æsthetic principles, it certainly lends itself to those of the international style.

The same is not so true of solid masonry. The character of masonry is in direct opposition to the character of contemporary methods of construction. Masonry, either of stone or brick, can hardly avoid offering an effect of mass and weight. Nor can it provide for large openings without the use of arches or of steel or ferroconcrete beams. Masonry structure used consistently throughout a building remains traditional both technically and æsthetically. Yet in monumental edifices which have only the most elementary functional requirements and demand the assurance of Egyptian permanence, masonry wall construction might appropriately be used. An exceptional monument of solid granite or marble of the order of the Temple of the Sphinx might be related to the international style by an imitative application of its æsthetic principles. The surface might be continuous, the detail minimal; but the effect of mass could hardly be honestly avoided.

IX

PLANS

Thus far there has been only incidental mention of the plan in contemporary architecture. Modern methods of skeleton construction have freed planning from conforming to the rigid lines of masonry structure. Isolated supports interfere hardly at all with free space and circulation. Interior partitions, like exterior walls, are mere screens. Thus planning has become absolutely pliant to the needs of function. New study of function, moreover, has broken down most of the conventions of planning inherited from the past, quite as rapidly as structural advance has made radical changes in plan possible.

The functionalists make a particular fetish of planning. They sometimes claim that they have never studied or composed their exteriors, but have merely allowed them to grow as the unavoidable clothing of the plan. It is true that the full application of the principle of regularity to the plans and the sections induces consistency in the elevations. It does not, however, lead automatically to good proportions in the façades. Architects who aim at achieving the fullest architectural character in their buildings must still study elevations alone quite as much as plans and sections.

The essence of architecture lies in the relation of the various sorts of geometrical projections. The realities of function influence chiefly the plan, but the expression of function must appear in the elevations. Even the functionalists who deny the necessity for æsthetic expression must admit that the essential character of the plan is generally apprehended from the exterior of the building. The contemporary exaggeration of the importance of the plan is primarily an architect's game. The game was well played at the Ecole des Beaux Arts long before modern architecture came into existence. It led to a very one-sided architecture since most of its interest and beauty could only be appreciated on paper.

The innovations in plan of the international style have led to much that is valuable both from the functional and from the æsthetic point of view. Even the functionalists have profited by the innovations of architects interested in the æsthetics of interior space. Today there are three types of interiors: first, the inside of the volume of the building, consisting of the entire content of the building or of a considerable part of it (Pages 109 and 220); second, interiors which open up into one another without definite circumscribing partitions (Page 190); and finally, the ordinary enclosed room.

The first sort of interior, which is not essentially different from the monumental interiors in the churches and theatres of the past, is of the scale of exterior architecture. Its walls are usually the interior surface of the same protecting screen which constitutes the exterior surface of the architectural volume. They require, therefore, a similar treatment, although naturally the demands of durability in the materials are much less stringent. In such interiors the supports will often stand isolated, making the character of the construction perfectly clear. These supports require different treatment, so that the lack of connection with the wall screens will be evident. They give scale to the created space. (Pages 109 and 220.) Therefore, they should be sharply defined and elegant in profile. Like the supports which are visible outside they are best if rounded in section.

The second sort of interiors is the particular invention of the international style. (Pages 146 and 194.) In contrast to the completely enclosed rooms of the past they stress the unity and continuity of the whole volume inside a building. The independence of the dividing screens and their variation in size and placing contrast with the regularity of the isolated supports. The flow of function and the relation of one function to another can be clearly expressed. The different screens serving different purposes may well be of different materials provided always their thinness and freedom from structural duty is stressed. While the visible supports give an underlying rhythm, the variety of the screens produce, as it were, a melody which may be restrained or lyric as the architect wishes. (Pages 122 and 186.)

The development of free planning, particularly with the use of curved and oblique screens, has been carried furthest in constructions of definitely architectural character. It gives to modern interiors a new kind of abstract space design unknown in the architecture of the past. But it is one of the elements of modern architecture which is easily abused, both practically and æsthetically.

Enclosed rooms of ordinary size, the third sort of interior, seldom have definite architectural character. They depend for their interest on their proportions and on their contents. (Page 208 f.)

Something has been said of the use of color in interiors, a matter subject far more to passing fashion than is color in exterior architecture. Screen walls should be, if possible, of natural materials in their own colors. If they are of plaster and painted, they should generally be white or neutral. Thin white curtains to moderate the light and heavier curtains of dark plain materials are harmonious and dignified. When drawn they cover the glass of the window wall with a temporary screen of fabric. In small enclosed rooms more use of artificial color is justifiable to give interest and variety; even, perhaps, different colors on different walls. But growing plants and fine pictures are the best means of giving life to interiors. The absence of all other decoration only gives them added emphasis and increases the importance of placing them properly in relation to the general design. The details of interior treatment will undoubtedly vary with the years far more than the general principles of the style.

X

THE *SIEDLUNG*[1]

The development of modern city planning has brought an increasing intervention of the political authorities in architecture. In some cases the æsthetic effect of this intervention has been for the good, substituting harmony for anarchical diversity, as in the buildings of Haussman's day which line the Paris boulevards. In other cases it is unfortunate, as in the case of the New York zoning law requiring the setback treatment of tall buildings; or in the case of the *Baupolizei* (building-police) in German cities, who

[1]The German word, *Siedlung*, serves more conveniently and specifically to denominate modern community housing projects than "garden suburb" or "residence subdivision."

force later builders on a street to continue the steep roofs used on the first houses.

But the state is more than a supervisor of architecture. It has itself become a patron of architecture in fields previously left to the individual. The state no longer erects only post-offices, schools and administration buildings. All over Europe public and semi-public agencies are concerning themselves with inexpensive housing. In America the patronage of housing developments by the state or by philanthropists, who so often carry on activities which are left to the government abroad, is only beginning.

Despite the development of group planning along modern lines in America the style of the individual houses in our "garden suburbs" remains traditional. Even where modern construction has been introduced, the sponsors have been loath to provide modern design. Hence our *Siedlungen* are sometimes excellent illustrations of sociological theory, but they are seldom examples of sound modern building and never works of architectural distinction.

Yet even housing at minimal cost is potentially architecture. The individual minimal dwellings provide for a function so simple and so little specialized that they are well within the realm of building and quite capable of standardization. But a project developed as a whole constitutes a complex problem offering so many opportunities for arbitrary choice that it may become architecture. American builders have standardized Tudor or Georgian forms and have produced extremely bad architecture, as cheap and meretricious as our modernistic skyscrapers. We may in the future standardize more fully and more logically by following the practice of European architects.

In the better *Siedlungen,* coördination offers a breadth of possibilities such as the mere repetition of similar buildings cannot give. The principle of regularity imposes a general order while the provisions for the different private and public functions of a complete *Siedlung* give variety and emphasis. The relation of the repeated units of actual housing to the special units serving the whole community is analogous to the relation in a hotel of the single guest rooms to the public rooms.

Gratuitous cultivation of asymmetry in the *Siedlung* is an offense against the principle of regularity. On the other hand, axial symmetry will seldom be possible throughout because of the necessities of proper orientation. (Page 158.) But the imposition of the same æsthetic disciplines on repeated units of housing and on special buildings will naturally give consistency to the whole composition.

Theatres, cafés, churches and schools will stand out. Because of their greater scale it is possible to give them a more architectural character than the ordinary surrounding buildings. Emphasized by the idiosyncrasies of their function, they symbolize group activities. Because they break the particular system of regularity of the surrounding housing, they constitute points of climactic interest. (Page 224.)

The *Siedlungen* of the European functionalists generally reach the neutral æsthetic level of good building, while the work of those who apply more consciously the disciplines of the contemporary style often rises to the level of architecture. The *Siedlungen* of the latter are not less practical. We must not be misled by the idealism of the European functionalists. Functionalism is absolute as an idea rather than as a reality. As an idea it must come to terms with other ideas such as that of æsthetic organization.

The modern *Siedlung* raises the question of what is meant by function in architecture more pertinently than does any other type of building. The general function is clear both in Europe and in America: to provide a large number of dwellings outside the city but still not too distant from the place of work of the inhabitants. Problems of communication, of retail merchandising and of entertainment are various, but they offer no field for architectural controversy. The more of such communal functions that can be incorporated in the same general plan, the more interesting and architectural will be the resultant *Siedlung*.

In the single residence units themselves the present and the future come to grips. In the case of a house built for a definite client and standing in its own grounds—still a very important architectural problem in every country of the world except Russia—the functions of the house as a place to live in must be worked out by the architect with the client. The man who is about to build a house knows his needs or can be forced to discover them by analysis. Indeed, satisfying the particular client is one important function of architecture that the European functionalists usually avoid. For them such work is without sociological significance.

The *Siedlung* implies preparation not for a given family but for a typical family. This statistical monster, the typical family, has no personal existence and cannot defend itself against the sociological theories of the architects. The European functionalists in their annual conferences set up standards for ideal minimal dwellings. These standards often have little relation to the actual way of living of those who are to inhabit them. Yet such theorizing has value as an instrument of social progress. Architects in private, as well as in public, practice must suggest and provide for the amelioration and development of the functions of living. They are specialists who can translate vague desires into realities. But there should be a balance between evolving ideal houses for scientific living and providing comfortable houses for ordinary living.

Too often in European *Siedlungen* the functionalists build for some proletarian superman of the future. Yet in most buildings the expressed desires of a given client are the most explicit and difficult functions. Architects whose discipline is æsthetic as well as functional are usually readier to provide what is actually needed. Their idealism is satisfied by raising their *Siedlungen* to the level of architecture by effective general planning and distinctive composition. The idealism of the functionalists too often demands that they provide what ought to be needed, even at the expense of what is actually needed. Instead of facing the difficulties of the present, they rush on to face the uncertain future.

There is a reverse side to this question of function in housing projects. It is frequently demanded by local critics that architects should cater to peculiar wants unknown in other communities. Windows arranged for strange forms of ventilation, or so subdivided that they may be opened without disarranging flower pots on the sill, rooms catering to special methods of drying clothes indoors, solid shutters on upper storeys to which no burglar could climb, certainly are needless unless local traditions insist upon them. In America, local traditions are further complicated by an excessive sentimentality about the "homes" of the past.

The architect has a right to distinguish functions which are major and general from those which are minor and local. In sociological building he ought certainly to stress the universal at the expense of the particular. He may even, for economic reasons and for the sake of general architectural style, disregard entirely the peculiarities of local tradition unless these are soundly based on local weather conditions. His aim is to approach an ideal standard. But houses should not be functionally so advanced that they are lived in under protest.

Whether the architects' work be a single elaborate country house, a public edifice, or a residence colony of apartments or small dwellings, the application of æsthetic principles of order, the formal simplification of complexity, will raise a good work of building to a fine monument of architecture. Whether the design be for a single filling station or for a whole city quarter, quality of architectural thought will count more than money spent on sites or on fine materials. If there be a choice of site, if there be money for chrome and marble, the beauty of natural surroundings and the beauty of rich smooth surfaces can only enhance the quality of architecture. An architecture, aristocratic rather than puritanical, may rise sometimes on an Acropolis in all the luxury of Pentelic marble and yet will grace with distinction the factory and the *Siedlung*.

Buildings will continue to be looked at as well as used. It is surely one function of architecture to provide for æsthetic appreciation. Fortunately the functionalists have not altogether failed to do so. Their achievements form an important part of the productions of the international style.

Within this style there are no subsidiary manners which are ecclesiastical or domestic or industrial. The symbolic expression of function by allusion to the past, which the half-modern architects at the beginning of the century developed, has ceased to be necessary. Where function is straightforwardly expressed, one type of building will not be confounded with another. Nor need that individuality break the premises of the style. The international style is broad and elastic enough for many varying talents and for many decades of development.

We have, as the Egyptians had or the Chinese, as the Greeks and our own ancestors in the Middle Ages before us, a style which orders the visible manifestation of a certain close relationship between structure and function. Regardless of specific types of structure or of function, the style has a definable æsthetic. That æsthetic, like modern technics, will develop and change; it will hardly cease to exist. It is found in the humblest buildings, as well as in monuments, fully architectural. Those who have buried architecture, whether from a thwarted desire to continue the past or from an over-anxiety to modify and hurry on the future, have been premature: We have an architecture still.

An appendix by Henry-Russell Hitchcock entitled "The International Style Twenty Years After" begins on page 239 following the plates.

Alvar Aalto: Turun Sanomat Building, Åbo, Finland. 1930 Newspaper Presses
INDUSTRIAL BUILDING RAISED TO THE LEVEL OF ARCHITECTURE BY FINE PROPORTIONS, SMOOTH SURFACES AND CAREFULLY STUDIED FORMS. THE SHAPE OF THE CONCRETE SUPPORTS EXPRESSES FRANKLY THE STRUCTURAL STRESSES.

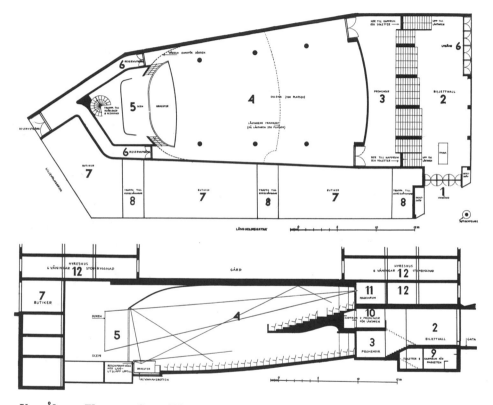

Uno Åhren: Flamman Soundfilm Theatre, Stockholm. 1929

ACOUSTICAL CONSIDERATIONS DETERMINE THE SHAPE OF THE INTERIOR. THE POSTS
APPEAR AS MERE LINES OF SUPPORT. LIGHTING FIXTURES ALONE DECORATE.

Josef Albers: Living Room in the Berlin Building Exposition. 1931
WOODEN CHAIRS DESIGNED WITHOUT REFERENCE TO TRADITION. THE COLOR
THROUGHOUT IS THAT OF THE NATURAL MATERIALS.

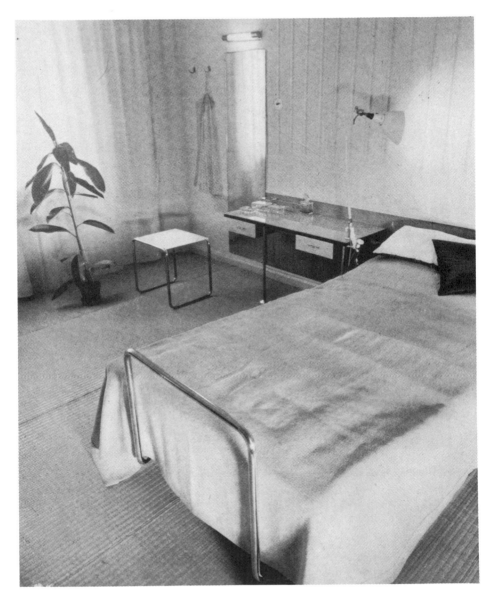

Marcel Breuer: Apartment Bedroom, Berlin. 1931

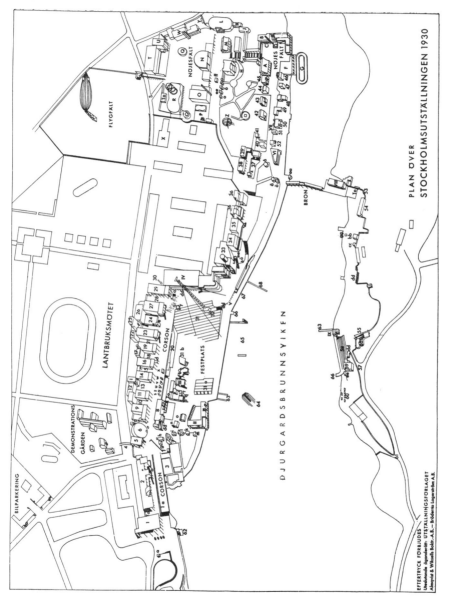

PLAN ÖVER

STOCKHOLMSUTSTÄLLNINGEN 1930

E.G. Asplund: Pavilions at the Stockholm Exposition. 1930

ASBESTOS SHEATHING AND LARGE WINDOWS IN LIGHT FRAMES PRODUCE AN EXCELLENT SURFACE FOR WOOD CONSTRUCTION. OFF-WHITE WALLS OF SIDE PAVILIONS CONTRAST WITH GREEN OF CENTER PAVILION. SKILFUL DECORATIVE USE OF LETTERING AND COLORED FLAGS.

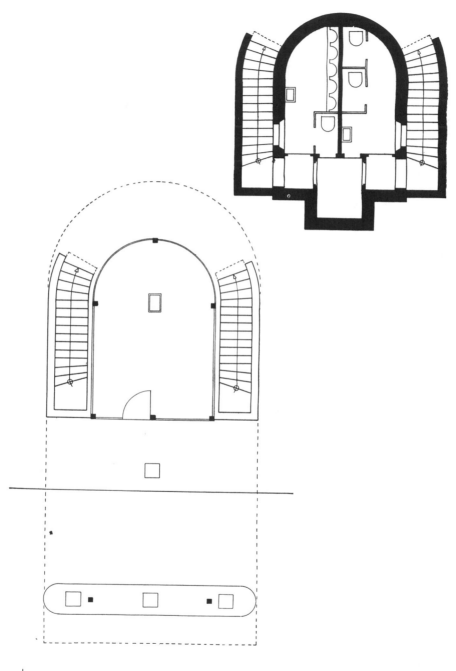

Hans Borkowsky: Dapolin Filling Station, Kassel, Germany. 1930

DOMINATING ROOF PLANE OVER TRANSPARENT SCREEN WALL. COLORS: BRILLIANT RED AND WHITE FOR ADVERTISEMENT. A DESIGN EASY TO STANDARDIZE. COMPARE WITH STANDARDIZED AMERICAN STATION ON PAGE 121.

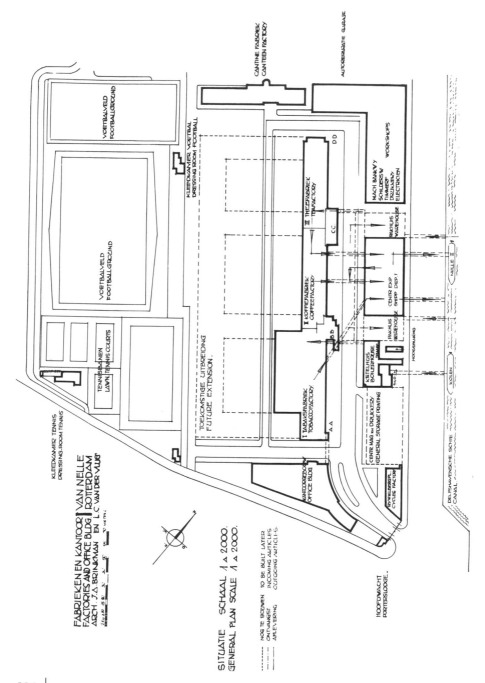

FABRIEKEN EN KANTOOR VAN NELLE ROTTERDAM
FACTORIES AND OFFICE BLDG.
ARCH. J.A. BRINKMAN EN L.C. VAN DER VLUGT

SITUATIE SCHAAL 1 : 2000.
GENERAL PLAN SCALE 1 : 2000.

--------- NOG TE BOUWEN   TO BE BUILT LATER
--- --- --- ONTVANGST   INCOMING ARTICLES
--- --- --- AFLEVERING   OUTGOING ARTICLES

VOETBALVELD
FOOTBALL GROUND

VOETBALVELD
FOOTBALL GROUND

KLEEDKAMER VOETBAL
DRESSING-ROOM FOOTBALL

CANTINE FABRIEK
CANTEEN FACTORY

AUTOGARAGE GARAGE

TENNISBANEN
LAWN TENNIS COURTS

KLEEDKAMER TENNIS
DRESSING-ROOM TENNIS

TOEKOMSTIGE UITBREIDING
FUTURE EXTENSION.

III THEEFABRIEK
TEAFACTORY

I KOFFIEFABRIEK
COFFEEFACTORY

I TABAKSFABRIEK
TOBACCOFACTORY

MACH. BANK v.v.
SCHILDERS W.
TIMMERW.
DRUKKERIJ
ELECTRICIEN

WORKSHOPS

PAKHUIS
WAREHOUSE

CENTR EXP
SHIPP DEP.T

PAKHUIS
WAREHOUSE

CENTR MAG EN DRUKKERIJ
GENERAL STORAGE PRINTING

KETELHUIS
BOILERHOUSE

HOOGSPANNING

KANTOORGEBOUW
OFFICE BLDG.

RIJWIELBERGPL.
CYCLES FACTORY

HOOFDWACHT
PORTERSLODGE.

DELFSHAVENSCHE SCHIE
CANAL

KOLEN

HALLE II

Brinkman & Van Der Vlugt: Van Nelle Tobacco, Tea & Coffee Factory, Rotterdam.
1928–30

An industrial building admirably composed of three sections, each devoted
to a separate function but with the same structural regularity throughout.

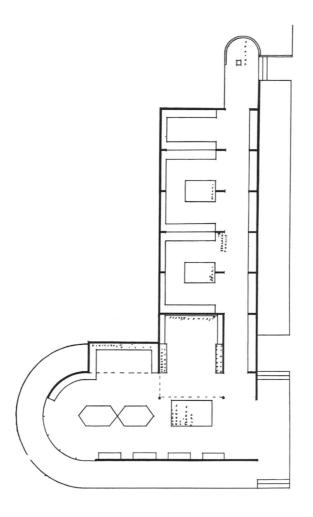

Erik Bryggman: Finnish Pavilion at the Antwerp Exposition. 1930

RICH SURFACES OF VARNISHED PLYWOOD. LETTERING USED EFFECTIVELY IN SILHOUETTE.

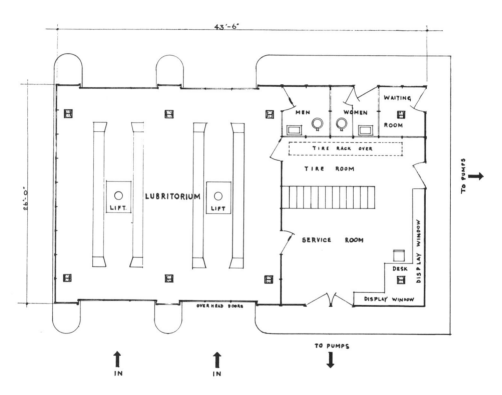

43'-6"

26'-0"

LUBRITORIUM

LIFT.   LIFT

MEN   WOMEN   WAITING

ROOM

TIRE RACK OVER

TIRE ROOM

SERVICE ROOM

DESK

DISPLAY WINDOW

DISPLAY WINDOW

OVERHEAD DOORS

TO PUMPS

TO PUMPS

IN   IN

THE STANDARDIZED PLAN

IN THE ILLUSTRATED STATION THE PLAN IS REVERSED AND SLIGHTLY MODIFIED.

120

Clauss & Daub: Filling Station, Standard Oil Company of Ohio, Cleveland. 1931

RED, WHITE AND BLUE COLOR DICTATED BY ADVERTISING. WHITE BAND UNDULY HEAVY.
GOOD LETTERING. ONE OF A SERIES OF FORTY STATIONS. ASYMMETRICAL PLACING OF
DOOR AND SHOP WINDOW AS SHOWN IN PLAN IS SUPERIOR TO THE ARRANGEMENT IN
THIS STATION.

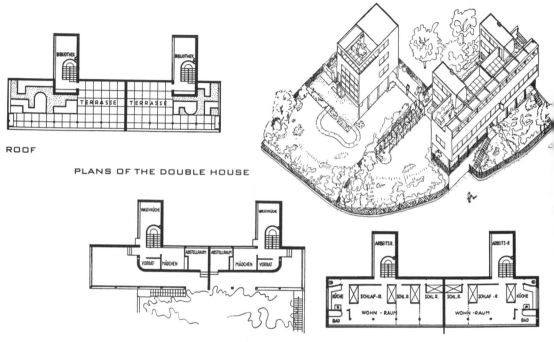

ROOF

PLANS OF THE DOUBLE HOUSE

GROUND FLOOR

MAIN FLOOR

Le Corbusier & Pierre Jeanneret: Single House and Double House at the Weissenhofsiedlung, Stuttgart. 1927

THE SINGLE HOUSE DERIVES FROM THE "CITROHAN" PROJECT OF 1921. THE DOUBLE HOUSE IS AN EXTREME EXAMPLE OF OPEN INTERIOR PLANNING. PROJECTING REAR WINGS DISTINGUISHED BY BEING PAINTED PALE GREEN. WINDOW ARRANGEMENT IS BRILLIANT AND DISCIPLINED.

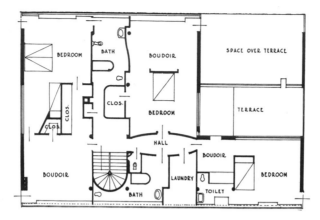

SECOND FLOOR

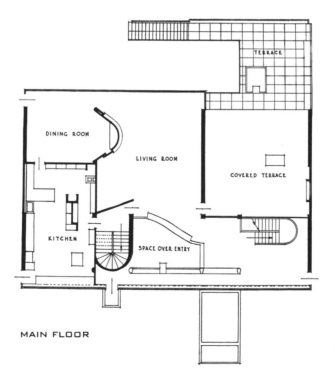

MAIN FLOOR

Le Corbusier & Pierre Jeanneret: Stein House, (Les Terrasses) Garches, Near St. Cloud. 1928

COVERED TERRACES, WHICH ARE INCLUDED IN THE SIMPLE RECTILINEAR VOLUME OF THE BUILDING, PRODUCE AN ASYMMETRICAL COMPOSITION. THE PREVAILING COLOR IS CREAM-WHITE. AT THE BACK OF THE TERRACES ONE WALL IS GREY AND ONE GREEN TO EMPHASIZE THE PLANES.

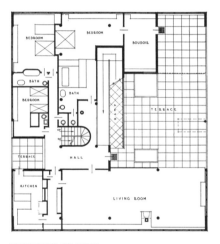

SECOND FLOOR   GROUND FLOOR

Le Corbusier & Pierre Jeanneret: Savoye House, Poissy-sur-Seine. 1930

THE WHITE SECOND STOREY APPEARS WEIGHTLESS ON ITS ROUND POSTS. ITS SEVERE SYMMETRY IS A FOIL TO THE BRILLIANT STUDY IN ABSTRACT FORM, UNRESTRICTED BY STRUCTURE, OF THE BLUE AND ROSE WINDSHELTER ABOVE. THE SECOND STOREY, AS SHOWN BY THE PLAN, INCLUDES THE OPEN TERRACE WITHIN THE GENERAL VOLUME. THUS THE SINGLE SQUARE OF THE PLAN CONTAINS ALL THE VARIED LIVING NEEDS OF A COUNTRY HOUSE.

Le Corbusier & Pierre Jeanneret: Savoye House, Poissy-Sur-Seine. 1931.
Living Room and Terrace

ONLY A SLIDING GLASS WALL SEPARATES THE LIVING ROOM FROM THE TERRACE. RAMP
AND CIRCULAR STAIRCASE, WITH THE RELATED PATTERNS OF WINDOW MUNTINS AND
RAILING, ARE SKILFULLY COMPOSED.

Le Corbusier & Pierre Jeanneret: Savoye House, Poissy-Sur-Seine. 1930. Hall

ARCHITECTURAL DETAIL ESPECIALLY FINE: THE RELATION OF ROUND PIER TO
SUPPORTED BEAM, THE CURVED PLANES OF THE STAIR, THE PLACING OF THE DOOR AND
ITS LIGHT ENFRAMEMENT.

Le Corbusier & Pierre Jeanneret: Lodge at Savoye House, Poissy-Sur-Seine. 1930

THE SMALL LODGE IS CONSISTENT IN DESIGN WITH THE MAIN HOUSE SHOWN ON THE
PREVIOUS PAGE. IT MIGHT WELL SERVE AS A UNIT DWELLING IN A HOUSING PROJECT.

Le Corbusier & Pierre Jeanneret: De Mandrot Villa, Le Pradet, Near Hyeres. 1931.
Living Room

SOUTH WALL OF TRANSPARENT, TRANSLUCENT AND OPAQUE PANELS, CEILING OF
PLYWOOD IN NATURAL COLOR AND FLOOR OF LOCAL TILES. FURNITURE BY RÉNÉ
HERBST AND HÉLÈNE DE MANDROT.

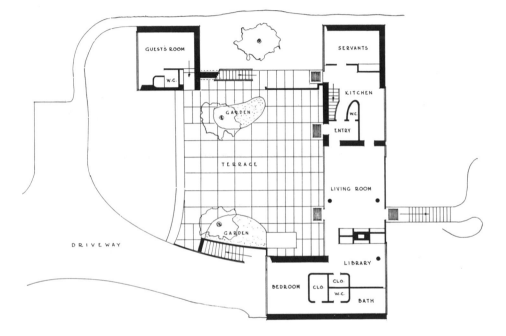

MAIN FLOOR

Le Corbusier & Pierre Jeanneret: De Mandrot Villa, Le Pradet, Near Hyeres. 1931

COMBINATION OF MASONRY AND ISOLATED POST CONSTRUCTION. NON-SUPPORTING WALL SECTIONS ARE OF STUCCO OR GLASS. BADLY PLACED WOODEN FLY-SCREEN FRAMES MAR THE FENESTRATION.

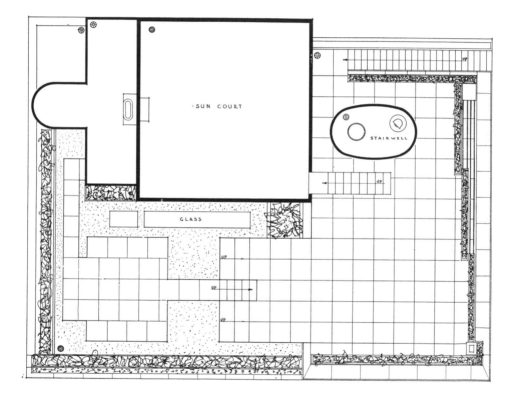

SUN COURT

GLASS

STAIRWELL

UP

UP

UP

UP

UP

Le Corbusier & Pierre Jeanneret: De Beistegui Pent House, Champs-Elysées, Paris. 1931. Garden

SIMPLE COMPOSITION OF RECTANGULAR FORMS AND OVAL STAIR TOWER. THE HEDGES AND THE TREE MAKE A STRIKING CONTRAST WITH THE WHITE MARBLE. THE HEDGES ARE SET IN SLIDING BOXES OPERATED ELECTRICALLY. THUS EITHER COMPLETE PRIVACY OR A MAGNIFICENT VIEW TOWARD THE CENTER OF THE CITY MAY BE ENJOYED. THE UPPER ENCLOSED AREA, A SUN BATH, HAS A FLOOR OF GRASS AND WALLS OF PALE SKY-BLUE.

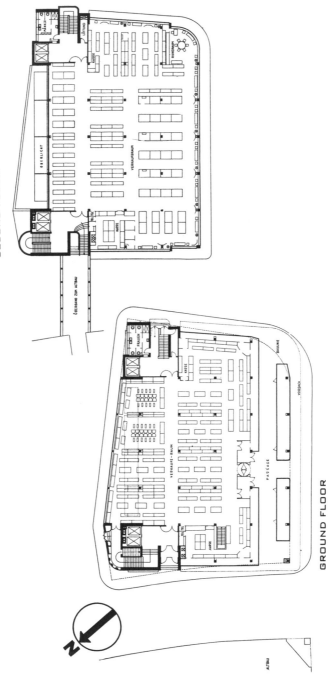

SECOND FLOOR

GROUND FLOOR

136

Eisenlohr & Pfennig: Breuninger Department Store, Stuttgart. 1931

THE WINDOW FRAMES ARE BRONZE AND THE WALLS ARE SURFACED WITH STONE
PLAQUES. THE SET-BACK IS BETTER HANDLED HERE THAN IN THE DEPARTMENT STORE
ON PAGE 185. CURVED CORNER AND LETTERING BREAK THE MONOTONY. THE DESIGN IS
DISCIPLINED BUT LACKS INDIVIDUAL DISTINCTION.

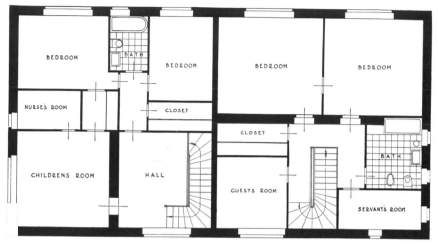

SECOND FLOOR

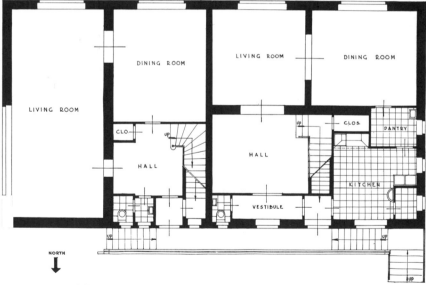

NORTH

GROUND FLOOR

Otto Eisler: Double House, Brno, Czechoslovakia. 1926

EFFECTIVE ASYMMETRICAL COMPOSITION. THERE IS TOO MUCH VARIETY IN THE SIZE AND SPACING OF THE FIRST FLOOR WINDOWS IN AN ATTEMPT TO ACHIEVE A PROGRESSIVE RHYTHM. THE THICK WINDOW FRAMES APPEAR EVEN HEAVIER BECAUSE THEY ARE LIGHT-COLORED INSTEAD OF DARK.

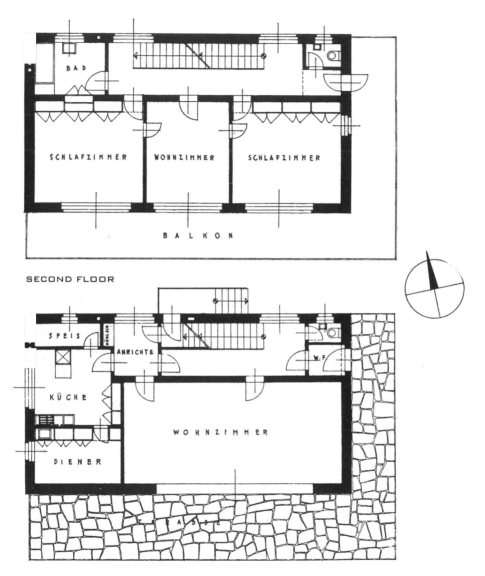

SECOND FLOOR

GROUND FLOOR

Otto Eisler: House for Two Brothers, Brno, Czechoslovakia. 1931

EXTREME REGULARITY RELIEVED BY THE ASYMMETRICAL SHELTER ON THE ROOF AND BY THE LARGE WINDOW ON THE GROUND FLOOR. THE PROPORTIONS ARE RATHER HEAVY BUT THE GENERAL EFFECT IS LIGHTENED BY THE BALCONY RAILING. SURFACED WITH RED ARTIFICIAL STONE.

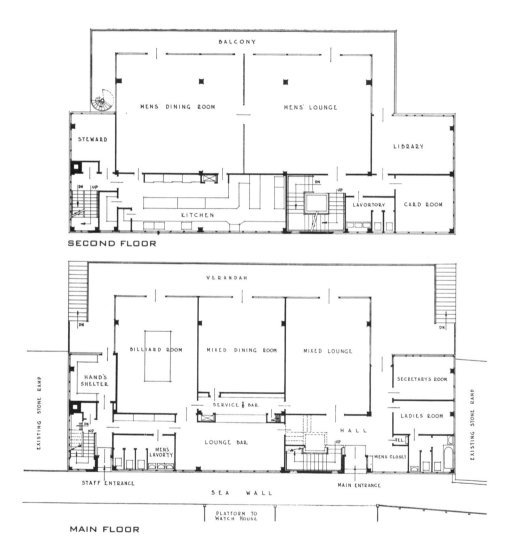

SECOND FLOOR

MAIN FLOOR

Joseph Emberton: Royal Corinthian Yacht Club, Burnham-on-Crouch, England.
1931

THE LARGE GLASS AREA IS PARTICULARLY SUITABLE IN A DULL, FOGGY CLIMATE.
COMPARE THE HOTEL IN CORSICA, PAGE 181, WHICH HAS SMALL WINDOWS TO KEEP
THE INTERIOR COOL AND DARK.

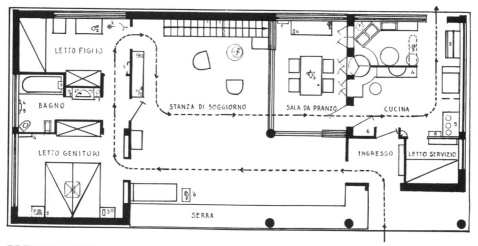

LETTO FIGLIO

BAGNO

LETTO GENITORI

STANZA DI SOGGIORNO

SALA DA PRANZO

CUCINA

INGRESSO

LETTO SERVIZIO

SERRA

GROUND FLOOR

L. Figini and G. Pollini: Electrical House at the Monza Exposition, Italy. 1930

THE SAME UNIT OF MEASURE IN WINDOW MUNTINS AND RAILINGS PRODUCES A
SUBSIDIARY RHYTHM.

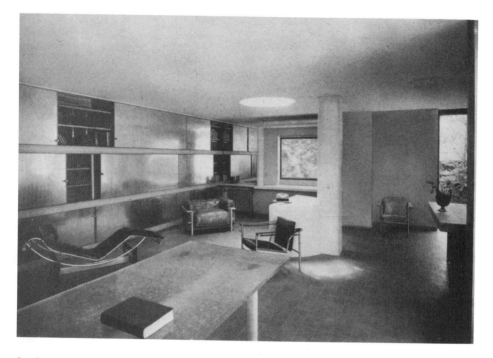

Le Corbusier & Pierre Jeanneret: Annex to Church Villa, Ville D'Avray. 1929. Living Room

PLACING OF FIREPLACE AND CHIMNEY AWAY FROM THE WALL AVOIDS THE TRADITIONAL MASSIVE EFFECT. STARTLING USE OF CIRCULAR SKYLIGHT. FURNITURE BY LE CORBUSIER AND CHARLOTTE PERRIAND.

***Bohuslav Fuchs: Pavilion of the City of Brno at the Brno Exposition, Czechoslovakia.
1928***

Piers and lintels of the substructure are unduly heavy. The circular
staircase is good decoration though its utility is doubtful. The windows
adjacent to the staircase are of glass tiles which harmonize in size with the
handsome orange red tile of the wall surface.

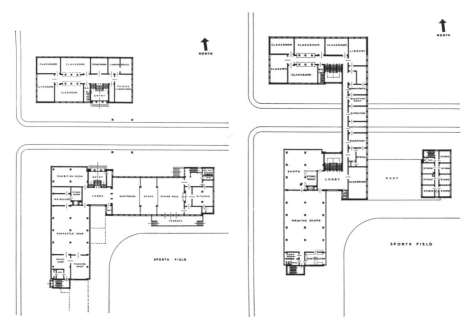

GROUND FLOOR   SECOND FLOOR

Walter Gropius: Bauhaus School, Dessau, Germany. 1926. Living Quarters, Administration and Class Rooms

THE SEPARATE WINGS, EACH WITH A DIFFERENT FUNCTION—LIVING QUARTERS, CLASSROOMS, WORKSHOPS—ARE SKILFULLY COMPOSED. THE CHECKERBOARD WINDOW ARRANGEMENT OF THE LIVING QUARTERS CONTRASTS WITH THE RIBBON WINDOWS OF THE CLASSROOMS AND ADMINISTRATIVE SECTION. AN EXAMPLE OF DIFFERENT FUNCTIONS EMPHASIZED BY A DIFFERENT HANDLING OF REGULARITY. THE SUPPORTS OF THE CENTER SECTION ARE AWKWARD IN SHAPE.

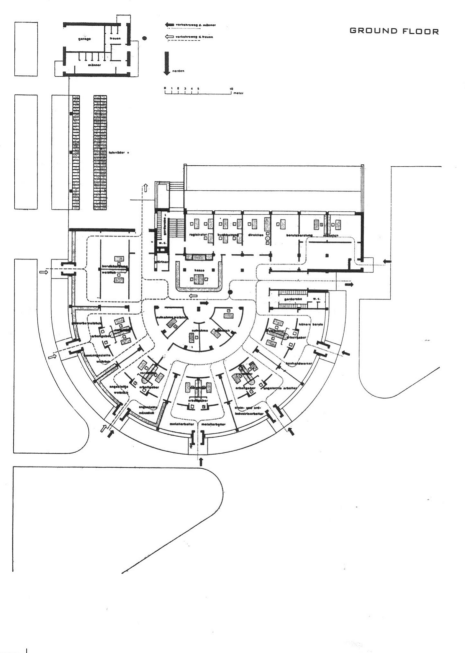

Walter Gropius: City Employment Office, Dessau, Germany. 1928

BRICK AS A WALL SURFACE USED SUCCESSFULLY WITHOUT TRADITIONAL FEELING.
ARCHITECTURAL DISTINCTION GIVEN TO A BUILDING OF MODERATE COST. SKILFUL
ASYMMETRICAL PLACING OF THE STAIR TOWER AND VERTICAL WINDOW.

TOP FLOOR

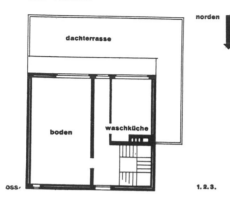

TYPICAL FLOOR

norden

1.2.3.

0 1 2 3 4 5   10 meter

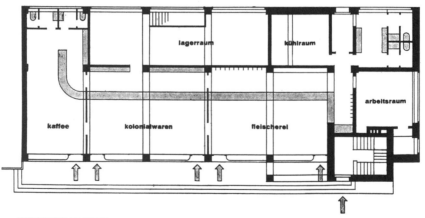

GROUND FLOOR

Walter Gropius: Siedlung Törten, Dessau, Germany. 1928. Coöperative Store &
Apartments

SHARP FUNCTIONAL CONTRAST BETWEEN HORIZONTAL DEVELOPMENT OF THE STORES
AND VERTICAL DEVELOPMENT OF THE APARTMENT HOUSE. LETTERING, CIRCULAR
WINDOWS AND FLAGPOLE ARE DECORATIVE ELEMENTS. THE TOP BALCONY IS
UNNECESSARILY HEAVY.

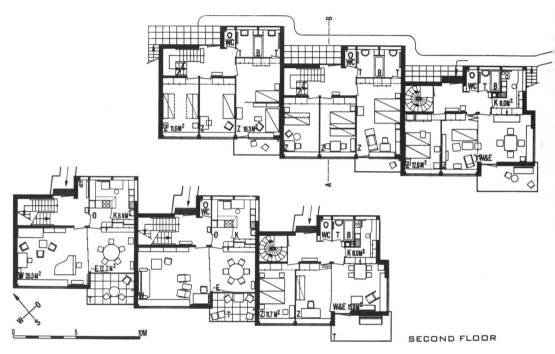

SECOND FLOOR

154

Max Ernst Haefeli: Apartment House, Zürich. 1929

PRONOUNCED WALL CAPPING AND ROUGH STUCCO BREAK THE EFFECT OF SURFACE. ALUMINUM WINDOW FRAMES ARE LIGHT AND WELL GROUPED. THE ENTRANCE BRIDGES MAKE GOOD DECORATION.

Walter Gropius: Bauhaus School, Dessau, Germany. 1926. Workshops

THE WORKSHOPS HAVE ENTIRELY TRANSPARENT WALLS. A GOOD ILLUSTRATION OF GLASS PANES AS A SURFACING MATERIAL. THE PROJECTION OF THE ROOF CAP IS UNFORTUNATE, ESPECIALLY OVER THE ENTRANCE AT LEFT.

Otto Haesler: Kurzag Warehouse and Offices, Brunswick, Germany. 1930
THOROUGH APPLICATION OF THE PRINCIPLES OF CONTEMPORARY DESIGN. THE
SYMMETRY IS FUNCTIONALLY JUSTIFIABLE SINCE THE STAIRWELL SERVES CENTRAL
CORRIDORS.

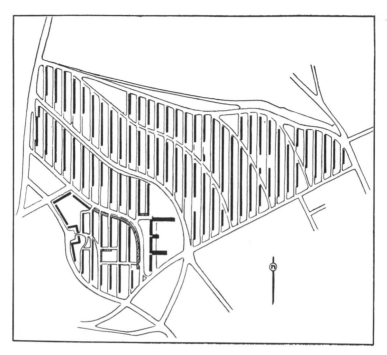

PLAN OF SIEDLUNG

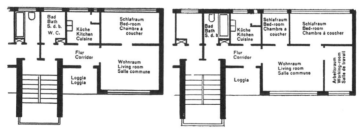

TYPICAL PLANS

158

Otto Haesler: Siedlung Rothenberg, Kassel, Germany. 1930

THE LONG BANDS OF WINDOWS ARE MADE POSSIBLE BY STEEL CONSTRUCTION. THE
INSET BALCONIES AND THE THICK CAPPING OF THE STAIRWELLS BREAK THE REGULAR
FENESTRATION DISAGREEABLY. THE STEPPING OF THE ROOF LINE, ON THE OTHER HAND,
GIVES AN INTERESTING VARIETY TO THE GENERAL SYSTEM OF REGULARITY.

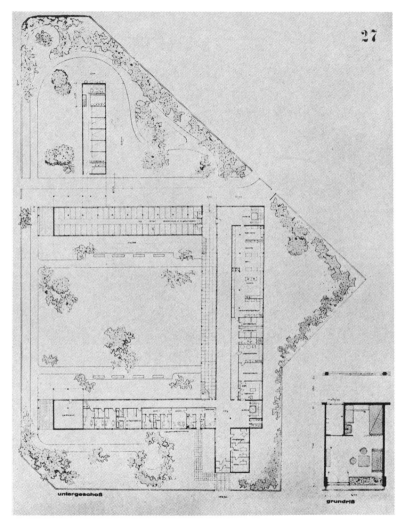

untergeschoß   grundriß

GROUND FLOOR   TYPICAL APARTMENT

Otto Haesler and Karl Völker: Old People's Home, Kassel, Germany. 1931

THE TALL SECTIONS ARE BUILT UP OF REPEATED UNITS OF LIVING QUARTERS. THE LOW
SECTION IN THE CENTER CONTAINS THE COMMON ROOMS; THE LOW SECTION TO THE
RIGHT, THE SERVICE QUARTERS. THESE VARIOUS DIVISIONS, EACH RETAINING ITS
DISTINCTIVE CHARACTER, ARE BROUGHT INTO AN ORDERLY COMPOSITION. THE
OCCASIONAL VERTICALS OF THE STAIRWELLS CONTRAST WITH THE GENERAL
HORIZONTALITY.

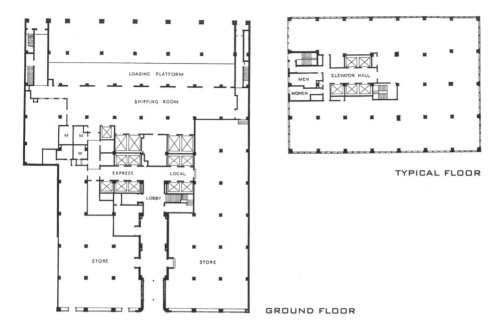

LOADING PLATFORM

SHIPPING ROOM

EXPRESS   LOCAL

LOBBY

STORE   STORE

GROUND FLOOR

MEN   ELEVATOR HALL

WOMEN

TYPICAL FLOOR

Hood & Foulhoux: McGraw-Hill Building, West 42nd Street, New York. 1931

THE LIGHTNESS, SIMPLICITY AND LACK OF APPLIED VERTICALISM MARK THIS
SKYSCRAPER AS AN ADVANCE OVER OTHER NEW YORK SKYSCRAPERS AND BRING IT
WITHIN THE LIMITS OF THE INTERNATIONAL STYLE. THE SPANDRELS ARE SHEATHED WITH
BLUE-GREEN TILES. THE METAL COVERING OF THE SUPPORTS IS PAINTED DARK GREEN.
THE SET-BACKS ARE HANDLED MORE FRANKLY THAN IN OTHER SKYSCRAPERS, THOUGH
STILL REMINISCENT OF THE PYRAMIDAL SHAPE OF TRADITIONAL TOWERS. THE
REGULARITY APPROACHES MONOTONY EXCEPT FOR THESE SET-BACKS, WHICH ARE
DETERMINED BY LEGAL REQUIREMENTS RATHER THAN BY CONSIDERATIONS OF DESIGN.
THE HEAVY ORNAMENTAL CROWN IS AN ILLOGICAL AND UNHAPPY BREAK IN THE
GENERAL SYSTEM OF REGULARITY AND WEIGHTS DOWN THE WHOLE DESIGN.

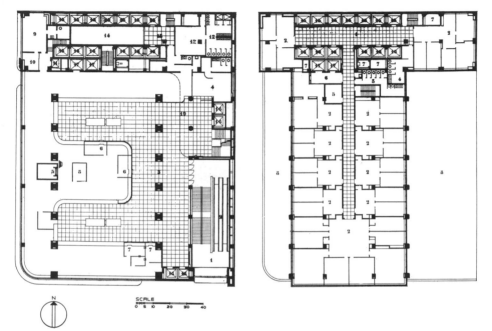

Howe & Lescaze: Philadelphia Saving Fund Society, Market Street, Philadelphia.
1931

THE BUILDING WILL NOT BE COMPLETED UNTIL THE SUMMER OF 1932. THE ENTIRE
FRONT IS CANTILEVERED. THE RELATION OF THE BASE WITH ITS CURVED CORNER TO THE
TOWER IS AWKWARD. THE DIFFERENT PARTS OF THE BUILDING ARE DISTINGUISHED BY
DIFFERENT SURFACING MATERIALS: THE BASE, HOUSING THE BANK, OF GRANITE SLABS;
TWO INTERMEDIATE STOREYS OF LIMESTONE; THE SPANDRELS OF THE TOWER OF BRICK.

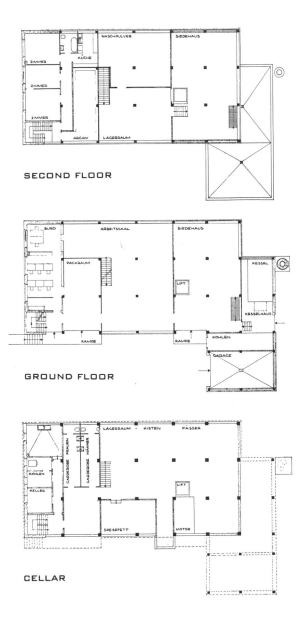

SECOND FLOOR

GROUND FLOOR

CELLAR

Kellermüller & Hofmann: Jakob Kolb Soap Factory, Zürich. 1930

A LOW-COST BUILDING GIVEN ARCHITECTURAL CHARACTER BY THE DISTRIBUTION OF THE
SECTIONS AND THE SPACING OF THE STANDARDIZED WINDOWS. THE DOORS ARE
UNFORTUNATELY NOT COMPOSED OF THE SAME UNITS AS THE WINDOWS.

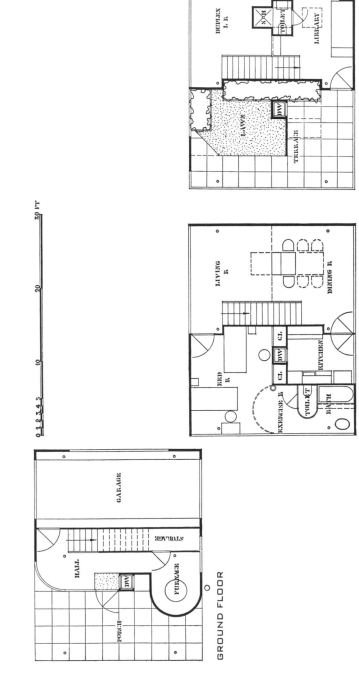

THIRD FLOOR

SECOND FLOOR

GROUND FLOOR

0 1 2 3 4 5   10   20   30 FT

A. Lawrence Kocher & Albert Frey: Harrison House, Syosset, Long Island. 1931

AN EXPERIMENTAL HOUSE WITH A SKELETON OF ALUMINUM AND WITH WALLS THINNER
THAN ARE PERMITTED BY URBAN BUILDING LAWS. CORRUGATED ALUMINUM SHEATHING
REFLECTS THE SURROUNDINGS AGREEABLY.

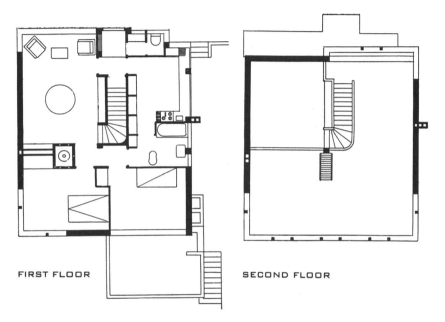

FIRST FLOOR   SECOND FLOOR

H. L. de Koninck: Lenglet House, Uccle, Near Brussels. 1926

THE PLANE OF THE WALL IS UNBROKEN EITHER BY WINDOW REVEALS OR WALL
CAPPING.

Josef Kranz: Café Era, Brno, Czechoslovakia. 1929

SKILFUL GROUPING OF WINDOWS WITH THE DIFFERENT FUNCTIONS OF VENTILATION, VIEW AND LIGHTING. LIGHT IS PROVIDED IN THE STAIRWELL BY THE USE OF TRANSLUCENT GLASS BRICKS. THE GENERAL COMPOSITION IS OVERCOMPLICATED.

Ludvik Kysela: Bata Shoe Store, Prague, Czechoslovakia. 1929

THE WINDOW FRAMES ARE LIGHT; THE SPANDRELS UNUSUALLY THIN. THE LETTERING IS BOTH UNARCHITECTURAL IN CHARACTER AND INHARMONIOUS IN SCALE.

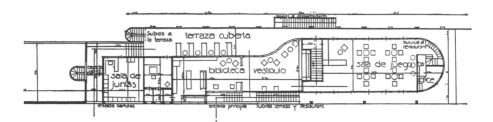

Labayen & Aizpurua: Clubhouse, San Sebastian, Spain. 1929

THE MARINE CHARACTER OF THE DESIGN IS JUSTIFIED BY SITE AND PURPOSE. THE
PROJECTION OF THE TERRACE ROOF ADDS AN UNNECESSARY COMPLICATION. COMPARE
EMBERTON'S SIMPLER TREATMENT OF THE SAME PROBLEM ON PAGE 146.

J. W. Lehr: Volksstimme Building, Frankfort, Germany. 1929

GOOD USE OF GLAZED TILE LAID VERTICALLY. THE WALLS ARE OFF-WHITE. PROJECTING SHELTER FOR NEWSPAPER NOTICES IS GREY WITH A BRILLIANT ORANGE POST.

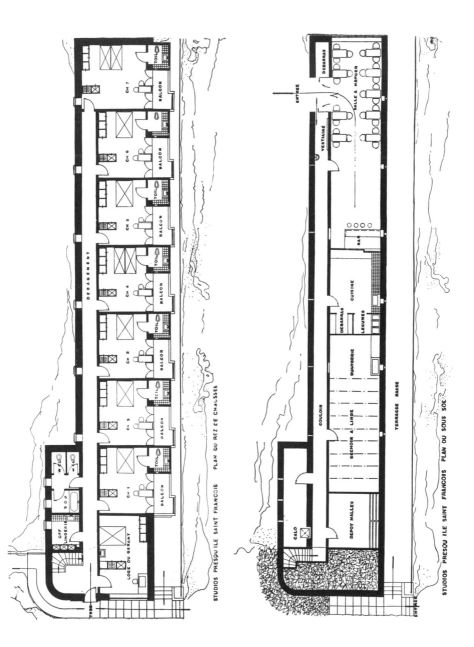

STUDIOS PRESQU ILE SAINT FRANCOIS   PLAN DU REZ DE CHAUSSÉE

STUDIOS PRESQU ILE SAINT FRANCOIS   PLAN DU SOUS SOL

176

André Lurçat: Hotel Nord-Sud, Calvi, Corsica. 1931

SMALL WINDOWS KEEP THE INTERIOR COOL IN A SEMI-TROPICAL SUMMER. THE PROJECTIONS BETWEEN THE BALCONIES ISOLATE THE SEPARATE STUDIO APARTMENTS.

THIRD FLOOR

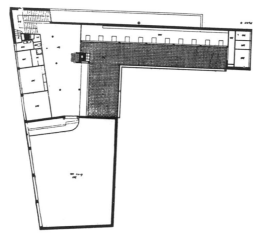

SECOND FLOOR

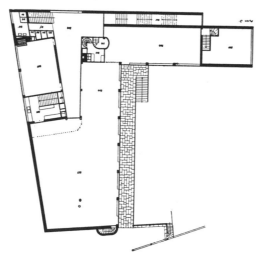

Sven Markelius & Uno Åhren: Students' Clubhouse, Stockholm. 1930. Roof Terrace

SUCCESSFUL DESIGN SAVE FOR THE THICKNESS OF THE WOODEN WINDOWS AND WALL CAPPING.

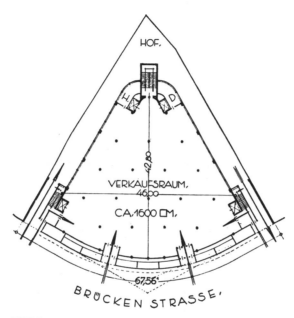

GROUND FLOOR

Erich Mendelsohn: Schocken Department Store, Chemnitz, Germany. 1928–1930

STARTLING RIBBON WINDOWS MADE POSSIBLE BY CANTILEVER CONSTRUCTION. WALL
SURFACED WITH STONE PLAQUES. THE SET-BACKS REQUIRED BY BUILDING LAWS GIVE
AN UNFORTUNATE STEPPED EFFECT, AS IN NEW YORK SKYSCRAPERS.

Erich Mendelsohn & R. W. Reichel: German Metal Workers' Union Building, Berlin.
1929–1930. Court

THE PHOTOGRAPH TAKEN THROUGH A WINDOW LIKE THOSE ACROSS THE COURT SHOWS
THE EXTREME LIGHTNESS OF THE FRAMES. THE STAIR TOWER IS UNSATISFACTORY IN
PLACING AND PROPORTION.

Theodor Merrill: Königsgrube Mine Works, Bochum, Germany. 1930

AN EXAMPLE OF REVEALED FRAMEWORK WHICH EXCEPT AT GREAT SCALE IS LESS
SATISFACTORY THAN THE USUAL METHOD OF SHEATHING THE FRAME.

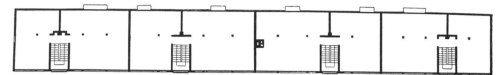

CONSTRUCTION PLAN FOR ALL FLOORS

THIRD FLOOR

SECOND FLOOR

FIRST FLOOR

Miës van der Rohe: Apartment House, Weissenhofsiedlung, Stuttgart. 1927
ALTHOUGH SYMMETRICAL, THE COMPOSITION DEPENDS FOR ITS EFFECT ON GENERAL
REGULARITY, NOT ON AXIAL EMPHASIS. SUPPORTS BETWEEN WINDOWS TREATED AS
PART OF THE WALL SURFACE. DESPITE SEVERE REGULARITY OF CONSTRUCTION THERE
IS GREAT VARIETY IN THE PLANNING OF THE INDIVIDUAL APARTMENTS.

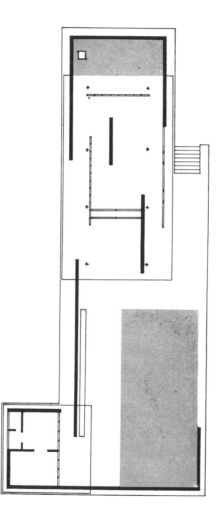

Miës van der Rohe: German Pavilion at the Barcelona Exposition, Spain. 1929

AS THIS WAS A PAVILION AT AN EXPOSITION, ÆSTHETIC RATHER THAN FUNCTIONAL CONSIDERATIONS DETERMINED THE PLAN. THE WALLS ARE INDEPENDENT PLANES UNDER A CONTINUOUS SLAB ROOF, WHICH IS SUPPORTED ON LIGHT METAL POSTS. THE ABSOLUTE REGULARITY IN THE SPACING OF THE SUPPORTS DOES NOT PREVENT WIDE VARIETY IN THE PLACING OF WALL SCREENS TO FORM SEPARATE ROOMS. RICH MATERIALS: TRAVERTINE, VARIOUS MARBLES, CHROME STEEL, GREY, BLACK, AND TRANSPARENT PLATE GLASS.

Miës van der Rohe: German Pavilion at the Barcelona Exposition, Spain. 1929. Inner Pool

BECAUSE OF DISTINCTIVE MATERIALS, THE PLANES RETAIN THEIR INDEPENDENCE. AS A RESULT THE COMPOSITION IS OF APPARENTLY INTERSECTING, RATHER THAN MERELY ENCLOSING, PLANES. THE DIFFERENT TEXTURES, INCLUDING THAT OF THE WATER, PROVIDE DECORATION. THE KOLBE STATUE HAS A MAGNIFICENT BACKGROUND AND THOUGH ISOLATED IS AN IMPORTANT PART OF THE DESIGN.

Miës van der Rohe: Lange House, Krefeld, Germany. 1928

UNUSUAL AND SUCCESSFUL USE OF BRICK IN A BUILDING WELL ABOVE AVERAGE COST.
THE TERRACE, LAID OUT GEOMETRICALLY, CONTRASTS WITH THE GROUNDS WHICH ARE
PLANTED NATURALISTICALLY.

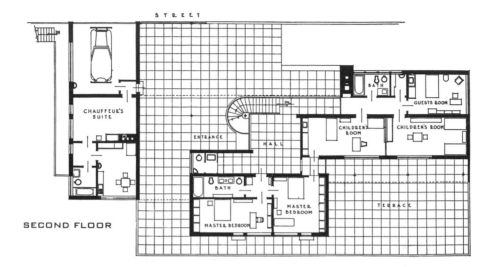

SECOND FLOOR

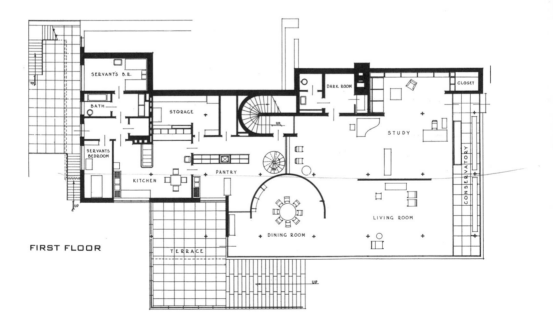

FIRST FLOOR

Miës van der Rohe: Tugendhat House, Brno, Czechoslovakia. 1930. Garden Façade

A CANTILEVERED PARAPET ONE HUNDRED FEET LONG ABOVE A WALL OF GLASS IS THE BASIS OF THE DESIGN. THE HOUSE IS TIED TO ITS SETTING BY A MONUMENTAL FLIGHT OF STEPS.

Miës van der Rohe: Tugendhat House, Brno, Czechoslovakia. 1930. *Street Façade*

THE HOUSE IS SO PLACED ON A SLOPING SITE THAT THE ENTRANCE IS ON THE SECOND
FLOOR. A SLAB ROOF ACROSS THE ENTRANCE JOINS THE GARAGE TO THE HOUSE. THE
CHIMNEY IS A STRONG VERTICAL ACCENT IN AN ALMOST WINDOWLESS FAÇADE.

Miës van der Rohe: Tugendhat House, Brno, Czechoslovakia. 1930. Entrance

A WALL OF FROSTED GLASS CURVED AROUND THE STAIRWELL LIGHTS THE ENTRANCE
HALL. SIMPLE BUT LUXURIOUS ELEMENTS OF DECORATION: THE ISOLATED BRONZE
POST, BRONZE WINDOW FRAMES, REFLECTING SURFACE OF GLASS, THE PATTERN OF
TRAVERTINE PAVING, THIN ROOF CAPPING, THE GRACEFUL RAILING AND GROWING
PLANTS.

Miës van der Rohe: Tugendhat House, Brno, Czechoslovakia. 1930. Library & Living Room

AN ONYX SPUR WALL SEPARATES THE LIBRARY ON THE LEFT FROM THE DRAWING ROOM ON THE RIGHT, BUT DOES NOT INTERFERE WITH THE OPEN FEELING OF ONE LARGE ROOM. BLACK OR WHITE VELVET CURTAINS ON CHROME RAILS CAN SEPARATE THE ROOMS MORE COMPLETELY; CURTAINS CAN ALSO BE DRAWN ACROSS THE GLASS WALLS. THE SUBDUED COLOR SCHEME—TAN, BEIGE, GREEN, PEARL GREY, WHITE AND BLACK—EMPHASIZES THE RICHNESS OF THE ONYX AND MACASSAR WOOD, THE BRILLIANCE OF THE CHROME POSTS AND PLATE GLASS.

Miës van der Rohe: Apartment Study, New York. 1930

VARIETY OF SURFACES—WINDOW WALL COVERED BY BLUE RAW SILK CURTAIN, A WALL OF
BOOKS ON PALISSANDER SHELVES, WHITE PLASTER CEILING, AND STRAW MATTING ON
THE FLOOR. CHAIR OF WHITE VELLUM, DESK OF BLACK LEATHER. ALL SUPPORTS OF
CHROME STEEL.

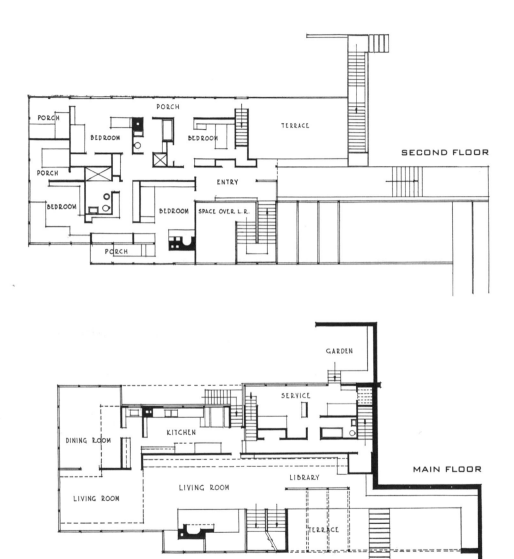

SECOND FLOOR

PORCH

PORCH

BEDROOM

PORCH

BEDROOM

BEDROOM

PORCH

TERRACE

ENTRY

BEDROOM

SPACE OVER L.R.

PORCH

GARDEN

SERVICE

DINING ROOM

KITCHEN

MAIN FLOOR

LIVING ROOM

LIBRARY

LIVING ROOM

TERRACE

N

196

Richard J. Neutra: Lovell House, Los Angeles. 1929

THE DESIGN, THOUGH COMPLICATED BY THE VARIOUS PROJECTIONS AND THE
CONFUSING USE OF METAL AND STUCCO SPANDRELS, IS BASED ON A VISIBLE
REGULARITY OF STRUCTURE.

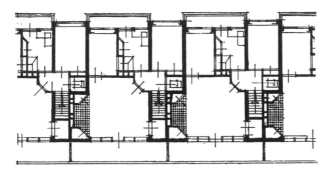

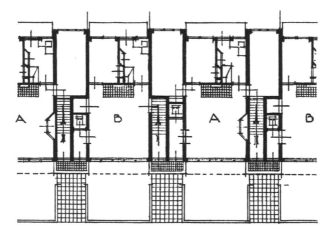

GROUND FLOOR

J. J. P. Oud: Workers' Houses, Hook of Holland. 1924–1927

THE CONTINUOUS BALCONY CARRIED AROUND THE CURVED SHOPS UNDERLINES THE
SIMPLE RHYTHM OF THE WINDOWS. THE DOWNWARD CURVE OF THE SHELTER
PROJECTION AND THE ADDED WALL CAPPING OVER THE SHOPS ARE PURELY
DECORATIVE.

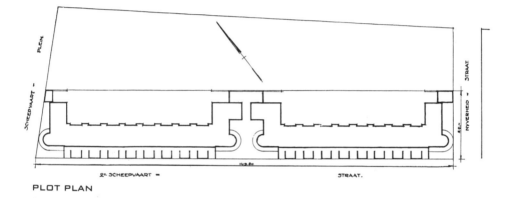

PLOT PLAN

J. J. P. Oud: Workers' Houses, Hook of Holland. 1924–1927. Shop

A SUBTLE COMPOSITION OF SIX CONCENTRIC CYLINDRICAL BANDS. THE THIN DISK OF
THE SHELTER, REPEATED IN THE DISK OF THE PAVEMENT BELOW, TERMINATES THE
GLASS WALL WITHOUT APPEARING TO WEIGH IT DOWN.

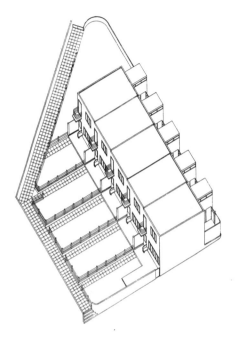

FIRST FLOOR

SECOND FLOOR

J. J. P. Oud: Row of Small Houses at the Weissenhofsiedlung, Stuttgart. 1927

THE PROJECTING BALCONIES AND THE SCREENS FOR VINES SEPARATING THE HOUSES
LIGHTEN THE DESIGN AND GIVE INTEREST TO THE REGULAR SCHEME. THE HOUSES ARE
STEPPED TO CONFORM TO THE GROUND SLOPE.

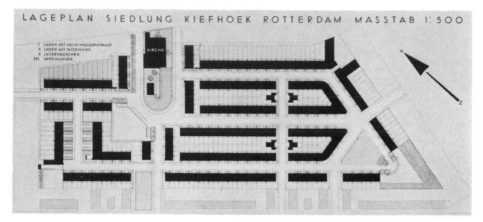

GENERAL PLAN

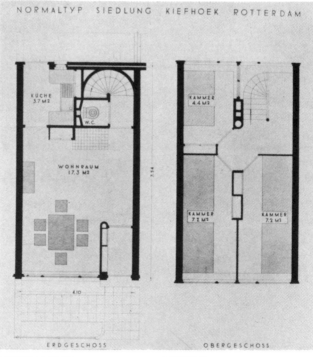

NORMALTYP SIEDLUNG KIEFHOEK ROTTERDAM

KÜCHE
3.7 M2

W.C.

WOHNRAUM
17.3 M2

7.54

4.10

ERDGESCHOSS

KAMMER
4.4 M2

KAMMER
7.2 M2

KAMMER
7.2 M2

OBERGESCHOSS

TYPICAL HOUSE PLANS   FIRST FLOOR   SECOND FLOOR

J. J. P. Oud: Siedlung Kiefhoek, Rotterdam. 1928–1930. Shops

EXTREME REGULARITY GIVEN INTEREST BY THE CURVES WHICH ALSO CONTINUE THE WALL SURFACE AROUND THE CORNER. THICK WOODEN WINDOW FRAMES ARE NECESSITATED BY INEXPENSIVE CONSTRUCTION. THEIR UNFORTUNATE HEAVINESS IS MINIMIZED BY THE TREATMENT OF THE WINDOWS AS A CONTINUOUS BAND OR SECOND STOREY WALL SCREEN.

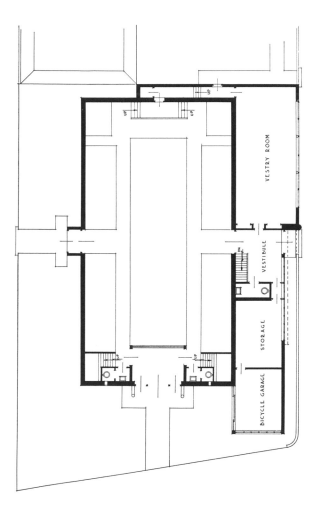

VESTRY ROOM

VESTIBULE

STORAGE

BICYCLE GARAGE

UP

UP

UP

UP

J. J. P. Oud: Siedlung Kiefhoek, Rotterdam. 1928–1930. Church

A COMMUNITY BUILDING OF SPECIALIZED FUNCTION WHICH FORMS THE HIGH POINT OF INTEREST IN A CONSIDERABLE AREA OF STANDARDIZED BUILDING. (SEE GENERAL PLAN ON PAGE 208.) THE SUBORDINATE ROOMS AND THE ROUNDED CHIMNEY SERVE AS ACCENTS TO THE SIMPLE RECTANGULAR BLOCK OF THE AUDITORIUM. LETTERING POOR AND BADLY PLACED.

Lilly Reich: Bedroom in the Berlin Building Exposition. 1931

LUXURIOUS AND FEMININE CHARACTER ACHIEVED BY COMBINATION OF WHITE
MATERIALS OF VARIOUS TEXTURES.

Jan Ruhtenberg: Apartment Living Room, Berlin: 1930

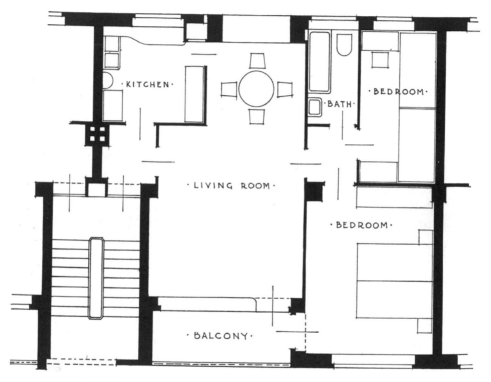

· KITCHEN ·

· BATH ·

· BEDROOM ·

· LIVING ROOM ·

· BEDROOM ·

· BALCONY ·

TYPICAL APARTMENT

Hans Schmidt (Artaria & Schmidt): Waldner House, Near Basle, Switzerland. 1930

CLEAR DESIGN MARRED BY BAD WINDOW DETAIL. COLOR IS CORAL RED.

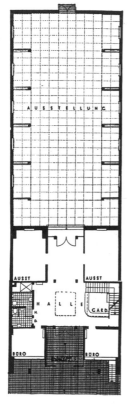

GROUND FLOOR

FOURTH FLOOR

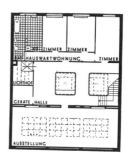

SECOND FLOOR

Karl Schneider: Kunstverein, Hamburg, Germany. 1930

A NINETEENTH CENTURY CITY HOUSE REMODELLED. THE SYMMETRICAL SOLUTION IS
HERE THE MOST FUNCTIONAL. THE LONG BAND OF RAISED LETTERING IS WELL USED
FOR DECORATION.

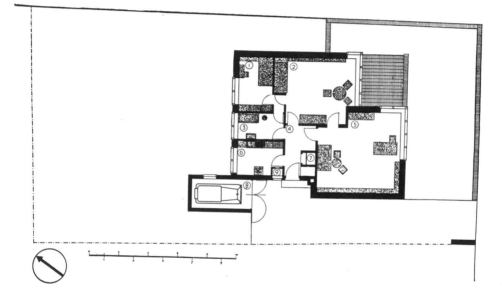

1. BEDROOM
2. BEDROOM
3. BATHROOM
5. LIVING ROOM
6. KITCHEN

Karl Schneider: Werner House, Near Hamburg, Germany, 1930

BRICKS WHEN LAID TRADITIONALLY SUGGEST MASONRY CONSTRUCTION, PARTICULARLY
ON SO SMALL A BUILDING. THE WINDOW FRAMES, INSET AT THE CORNERS, BREAK THE
VERTICAL EDGES.

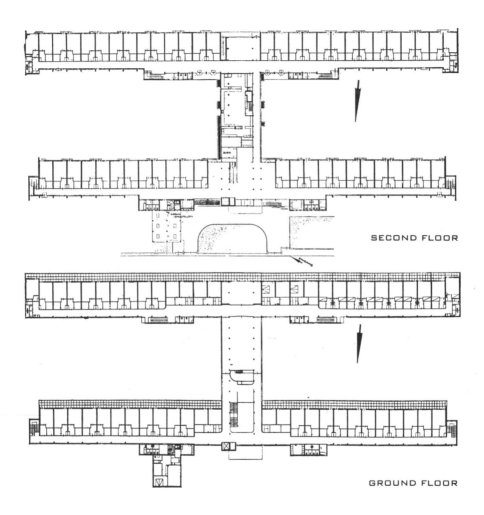

SECOND FLOOR

GROUND FLOOR

Stam & Moser: Budge Home for the Aged, Frankfort, Germany. 1929–1930
COMMON ROOMS CONNECT TWO WINGS OF ONE-ROOM APARTMENTS ORIENTED TO THE
SOUTH. THOUGH BUILT BY ARCHITECTS WHO CLAIM TO BE GUIDED SOLELY BY
CONSIDERATIONS OF ECONOMY AND FUNCTION, THE BUILDING HAS REAL ÆSTHETIC
MERIT AS WELL.

Stam & Moser: Budge Home for the Aged, Frankfort, Germany. 1929–1930. Lobby

WALL ABOVE BALCONY IS PALE BLUE AND THAT BELOW, BRIGHT RED. OTHER WALLS AND POSTS ARE WHITE. THE ROUNDED CORNERS ON THE PIERS ARE AN EXCELLENT REFINEMENT.

Mamoru Yamada: Electrical Laboratory, Ministry of Public Works, Tokio. 1929

A STRAIGHTFORWARD BUILDING WITHOUT MUCH REFINEMENT. THE ROUNDED EDGES
BLUR THE EFFECT OF VOLUME.

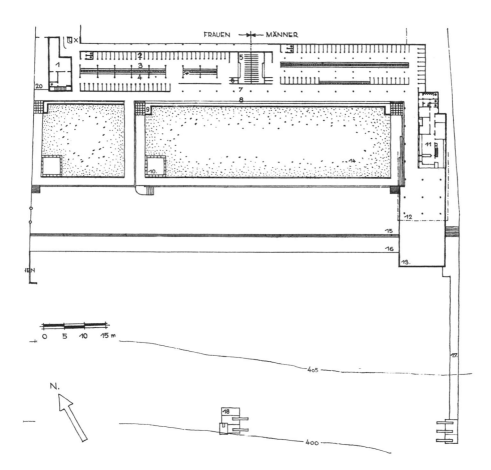

FRAUEN ←→ MÄNNER

Steger & Egender: Bathing Beach, Küsnacht, Near Zürich. 1928

THE RESTAURANT WITH ITS LONG THIN ROOF SLAB CONTINUES AS A TERRACE OVERLOOKING THE WATER.

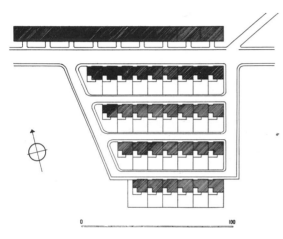

TYPICAL HOUSE

GENERAL PLAN

SECTION

***Eskil Sundahl: Siedlung of the Swedish Coöperative Society, Hästholmen, Near Stock-
holm. 1930***

ROWS OF WOODEN HOUSES FACING SOUTH ON A HILLSIDE. THE ROOFS ARE NOT FLAT
BUT THE PITCH IS MADE SLIGHT TO AVOID A GABLED EFFECT.

WORK BENCH

LAB LAB LAB STOVE LAB LAB LAB

MAIN LABORATORY

DARK ROOM AQUARIUM STORAGE

DIRECTOR'S
OFFICE

Tucker & Howell; Oscar Stonorov, Consultant: Biological Laboratory of the Highlands Museum, Highlands, N. C. 1931

PAINTED MATCH-BOARDING ADMIRABLY USED ON WOOD CONSTRUCTION. PIPE SUPPORT IS INCONGRUOUS AND APPEARS TOO FRAIL. WALLS ARE PALE LEMON YELLOW; BASE AND ENTRANCE ARE MAHOGANY RED.

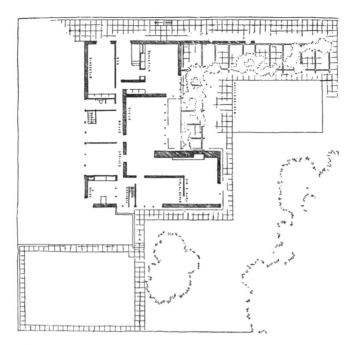

UPPER FLOOR

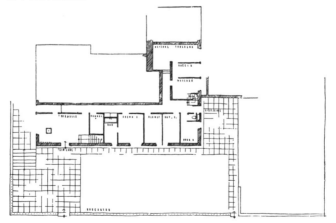

LOWER FLOOR

Lois Welzenbacher: Schulz House, Westphalia, Germany. 1928

UNFORTUNATE CONTRAST OF VERTICAL AND HORIZONTAL BRICK COURSES. INSTEAD OF
WINDOWS, THE LIVING ROOM HAS A WALL OF GLASS.

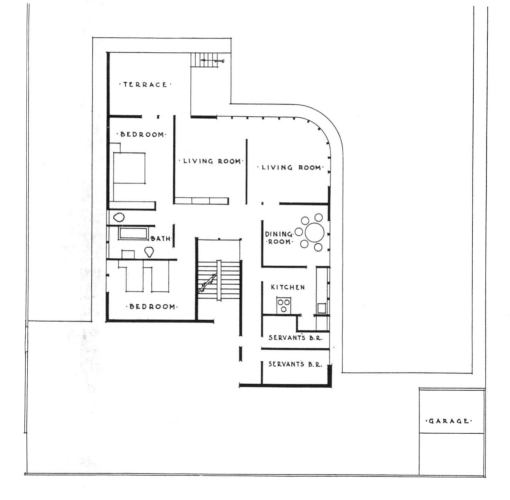

·TERRACE·

·BEDROOM·

·LIVING ROOM·

·LIVING ROOM·

·BATH

·DINING· ·ROOM·

·BEDROOM·

KITCHEN

SERVANT'S B.R.

SERVANTS B.R.

·GARAGE·

230

Lois Welzenbacher: Apartment House, Innsbruck, Austria. 1930

THE CURVED CORNER CANNOT BE JUSTIFIED BY FUNCTION NOR DOES IT APPEAR
NECESSARY TO THE DESIGN.

Essen, Office of the City Architect: Children's Clinic. 1930

THE PROJECTING WING TO THE LEFT PROVIDES A UNIFYING FRAME FOR THE
COMPLICATION OF THE SET-BACK SUN TERRACES.

Frankfort, Germany; Office of the City Architect (Ernst May): Friedrich Ebert School.
1931

ADJUSTMENT TO SITE GIVES LIGHT TO EACH ROW OF CLASSROOMS WITH THEIR GARDEN.

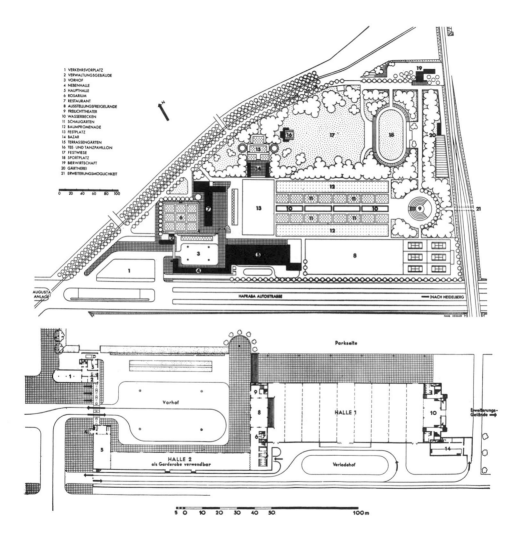

Mannheim, Germany; Office of the City Architect (Zizler & Müller): Exposition Buildings. 1930

SLANTED ROOF IS INGENIOUSLY, IF NOT HONESTLY, TREATED. GROUNDS AND
BUILDINGS SHOW THE INFLUENCE OF TRADITIONAL PLANNING ON SYMMETRICAL AXES.

Kassel, Germany: Office of the City Architect (Jobst), Savings Bank. 1931

A MUNICIPAL BUILDING, SOUND BUT NOT BRILLIANT IN DESIGN. LOWER LETTERING
BETTER PLACED THAN SILHOUETTED LETTERING ABOVE.

U. S. S. R., Government Architects (Nicolaiev & Fissenko): Electro-Physical Labora-tory, Lefortovo, Moscow. 1927

VERTICAL AND CURVED ELEMENTS USED WITH FUNCTIONAL JUSTIFICATION AND ÆSTHETIC SUCCESS.

Stuttgart, Architect of Postal Administration: Automatic Post Office. 1931

AN ADDITION, WITHOUT STYLISTIC COMPROMISE, TO AN OLD BUILDING. THE LINE OF THE
ROOF SLAB IS UNNECESSARILY COMPLICATED BY THE JOG AND THE CURVING CORNERS.

Appendix

A P P E N D I X

*T*he following article was written by H. R. Hitchcock for the August, 1951, Architectural Record. In form it is a series of quotations from the original 1932 text with comments made in the light of developments in modern architecture over the ensuing twenty years. Typographic differentiation indicates which are the quoted passages from the book—prepared in 1931, though published only the following year—and which are the comments of 1951.

The International Style Twenty Years After

The International Style was prefaced by a statement by Alfred Barr, the Director of the Museum of Modern Art. In his first paragraph he made a claim which the authors themselves might well have considered immodest:

> . . . They have proven beyond any reasonable doubt, I believe, that there exists today a modern style as original, as consistent, as logical, and as widely distributed as any in the past. The authors have called it the International Style.
>
> To many this assertion of a new style will seem arbitrary and dogmatic . . .

And how! A quarter century after Gropius's Bauhaus at Dessau and Le Corbusier's Pavilion de l'Esprit Nouveau at the Paris Exposition of Decorative Arts of 1925 first made evident that something like a concerted program for a new architecture existed, it is still by no means necessary to conclude that the "International Style" (which they and other European architects were then maturing) should be considered the only proper pattern or program for modern architecture.

The work of many architects of distinction such as Frank Lloyd Wright, who make no bones about their opposition to the supposed tenets of an International Style, certainly belongs to modern architecture as much as does the work of Gropius and Le Corbusier. Yet the particular concepts of a new modern style which date from the Twenties *do* conveniently define that crystallization—that convergence of long immanent ideas—which then took place in France and Germany and Holland, and which a quarter century later has spread throughout the civilized world. (Only, I believe, in Russia are the forms of the International Style unpopular—to put outright official proscription rather mildly!)

In general, it has been the concept of "style" itself, as implying restraint or discipline according to *a priori* rules of one sort or another, which has been hardest for architects, as distinguished from critics and writers, to accept. The introduction of the 1932 book was therefore devoted to defending "The Idea of Style" and this defense is still relevant—even if its validity is also still debatable—today:

> The chaos of eclecticism served to give the very idea of style a bad name in the estimation of the first modern architects of the end of the nineteenth and the beginning of the twentieth century.

The most distinguished older modern architects, notably Wright and Gropius, are still perhaps the most perturbed by the idea that anything that can properly be called a style, in the historic sense of that word, can have any worthwhile part to play in the architecture of the 20th century. Yet Wright himself obviously has a highly individualistic style—several, for that matter—and it is also obvious that that personal style (or those styles) of his could be utilized as a framework of architectural advance, if his precepts for "Organic Architecture" were widely accepted and conscientiously followed.

Gropius is proud of the fact that it is difficult to tell the work of one of his pupils from that of another—a difficulty that he in fact rather exaggerates. (For the work of Paul Rudolph, for example, differs a great deal from that of the members of what might be called the Boston Suburban School.) But what is this anonymity that the Chairman of the Harvard Department of Architecture admires in his pupils' work but a common style? It is not the "Gropius" or the "Bauhaus" style, moreover, but merely an important part of the broader International Style, as that is practiced by the third generation of modern architects in the North Eastern United States.

The individualistic revolt of the first modern architects destroyed the prestige of the [historic] "styles," but it did not remove the implication that there was a possibility of choice between one æsthetic conception of design and another.

To refuse a comparable liberty of choice today, merely because 25 years ago the development of modern architecture began to be notably convergent, is certainly a form of academicism. This is already only too evident in just the places one would expect to find it, that is, in prominent architectural schools and in large highly institutionalized offices. Modern architecture in the 1950s should have room again for a range of effects as diverse, if not as divergent, as Victor Horta's Maison du Peuple in Brussels of 1897, an early modern building largely of metal and glass that is too often forgotten now, and Wright's River Forest Golf Club (as first built in 1898), of ordinary wooden-frame construction, in which most of the concepts of his now "classic" prairie houses of the next decade were already almost fully mature.

The individualists decried submission to fixed æsthetic principles as the imposition of a dead hand upon the living material of architecture, holding the failure of the [stylistic] revivals [of the 19th century] as a proof that the very idea of style was an unhealthy delusion.

Much of what Dean Wurster has called "Drugstore Modern" suggests that the "individualists" were less completely in the wrong than we admitted 20 years ago. Certainly too rigid a concept of what is stylistically "permissible" is always stultifying. But throughout most of the intervening period our contention that:

The idea of style, which began to degenerate when the revivals destroyed the disciplines of the Baroque, has become real and fertile again.

has been supported by what has occurred.

The idea of modern style should remain, as it presently is in fact, somewhat loose rather than too closely defined. There will, however, always be some sort of style in the arts of self-conscious periods, whether it is so recognized, and so called, or not. Since it is impossible to return, under the circumstances of advanced civilization, to the unselfconscious production of supposedly styleless "folk arts," it is well to be aware that there *is* a problem of style. To attempt to dismiss style altogether is culturally ingenuous; it is also Utopian, or more accurately, millennial (in one sense at least, there were no "styles" in the Garden of Eden!).

The unconscious and halting architectural developments of the nineteenth century, the confused and contradictory experimentation of the beginning of the twentieth, have been succeeded by a directed evolution. There is now a single body of discipline, fixed enough to integrate contemporary style as a reality and yet elastic enough to permit individual interpretation and to encourage general growth.

Today that "fixing" is resented, just because it has been so successful. Yet the establishment of a fixed body of discipline in architecture is probably the major achievement of the 20th century, not any technical developments in building production that have become universally accepted; modern technical developments have recurrently disappointed the optimists and they have failed, perhaps even more conspicuously, to live up to the bolder prophecies of 19th century critics.

After 25 years, it is the "elasticity" and the possibility of "general growth" within the International Style which should be emphasized. That was already beginning to be evident to Philip Johnson and myself 20 years ago. Few of our readers, alas, seem to have given us credit for what were then readily dismissed as mere "escape-clauses."

The idea of style as the frame of potential growth, rather than as a fixed and crushing mould, has developed with the recognition of underlying principles such as archaeologists discern in the great styles of the past. The principles are few and broad.

Too few and too narrow, I would say in 1951 of the principles that were enunciated so firmly in 1932:

There is, first, a new conception of architecture as volume rather than as mass. Secondly, regularity rather than axial symmetry serves as the chief means of ordering design. These two principles, with a third proscribing arbitrary applied decoration, mark the productions of the international style.

Today I should certainly add articulation of structure, probably making it the third principle; and I would also omit the reference to ornament, which is a matter of taste rather than of principle. The concept of regularity is obviously too negative to explain very much about the best contemporary design; but I can still find no phrase that explains in an all-inclusive way the more positive qualities of modern design.

In opposition to those who claim that a new style of architecture is impossible or undesirable, it is necessary to stress the coherence of the results obtained within the range of possibilities thus far explored. For the international style already exists in the present; it is not merely something the future holds in store. Architecture is always a set of actual monuments, not a vague corpus of theory.

After twenty years there are many, many more "actual monuments" in existence; the results are still coherent, but the "corpus of theory" is both firmer and broader, if also harder to define. The mistake made by many readers of "The International Style" was—and if any one reads the book now, instead of depending on his memory or on second-hand reports of its contents, still is I fear—to assume that what the authors offered as a diagnosis and a prognosis was intended to be used as an academic rulebook.

It is an old story now, on the other hand, that Wright came very close indeed to the International Style in certain projects of the late 1920s, such as that for an apartment house for Elizabeth Noble in Los Angeles, and that many of his most famous later works, such as Falling Water, seem to include definitely "international" ideas. The architects of the San Francisco Bay Region, whom some critics have wished to build up as the protagonists of a more humanistic school opposed to the International Style, have also frequently followed its principles almost to the point of parody—although admittedly not in their best and most characteristic country-house work. Between these extremes of loose interpretation by one of the original definers of the International Style and of partial, or even at times complete, acceptance of its tenets by those theoretically most opposed to it, lies the great bulk of current architectural production.

Following the section devoted to "The Idea of Style" in the 1932 book came one on the "History" of modern architecture. We said then (rather condescendingly) of the architects active from 1890 to 1920:

Today it seems more accurate to describe the work of the older generation as half-modern.

In 1951 there seems no reason at all not to claim that the work of the older generation of modern architects was "early modern," not "half-modern." The achievements of the earlier men seem much greater today in retrospect, moreover, than they did 20 years ago. Without Wright's work of the last 20 years, it is hard to believe now that the full scope of his greatness could have been appreciated as it certainly had been in 1932 by many architects and critics for almost a generation. Yet it still seems a true enough historical statement to say that:

There was no real stylistic integration until after the war [of 1914–18].

The crystallization of what will perhaps in historical terms some day be called the "high" phase of modern architecture came in the 1920s. Now I suspect we are entering the "late" phase. Leaving that prognosis aside, much of what we wrote twenty years ago about the "early modern" architects still seems true.

Wright was the first to conceive of architectural design in terms of planes existing freely in three dimensions rather than in terms of enclosed blocks. Wagner, Behrens and Perret lightened the solid massiveness of traditional architecture, Wright dynamited it.

Such things as the interior of Otto Wagner's Postal Savings Bank in Vienna, of [1904–06], or Behrens's German General Electric turbine factory in Berlin, of [1909–10], appear today more extraordinary, in relation to what had preceded them in the previous century, than they did then.

Wright from the beginning was radical in his aesthetic experimentation.

Wright's Yahara Boat Club [Project], [for] Madison, Wisconsin, prefigured, well before Cubism reached maturity, most of the plastic innovations that contact with abstract painting and sculpture were to suggest, [many] years later, to the young European architects who initiated the International Style. The plan Wright prepared for a house to be built for himself in 1903, incorporating all the living areas except the kitchen in one articulated flow, is obviously an early prototype of the one-room houses that are frequently supposed to be a post-war development of the last five years.

Perret was, perhaps, a more important innovator in construction.

Perret's church at LeRaincy outside Paris, of 1923, remains more striking than much of the shell-concrete construction of the last decade. But Perret's later work has seemed less bold, both structurally and aesthetically, and he belongs in the main to the early 20th century. Wright's Johnson Wax Building in Racine, of [1937–39], particularly with the addition of the new laboratory tower completed last year, reveals on the other hand that the American architect's feats as an innovator in construction had not even reached their peak in 1932. If such buildings as Notre Dame du Raincy and the Racine structures are not prime examples of modern architecture, the word "modern" has no meaning. On the other hand, they certainly do not fit conveniently into the frame of the International Style as it was envisaged between 1922 and 1932.

With regard to the moment of stylistic crystallization in the 1920s I think it is still true to say, as we wrote in 1931:

> . . . the man who first made the world aware that a new style was being born was Le Corbusier.

Furthermore, no one has done more than Le Corbusier ever since to extend and loosen the sanctions of the International Style. That was already apparent in 1932 in his house for Mme. de Mandrot at Le Pradet, of 1931, and in his Errazuris house of the same date in Chile. It is in some respects perhaps less evident today, at least in New York, since the UN office building (in whose design he played some part) may be considered "early" Le Corbusier—like his Paris projects of the Twenties—rather than post-War Le Corbusier, at least in the form in which it has been executed.

> In [Le Corbusier's] Citrohan house models of [1919-] 1921 . . . the enormous window area and the terraces made possible by the use of ferro-concrete, together with the asymmetry of the composition, undoubtedly produced a design more thoroughly infused with new spirit, more completely freed from the conventions of the past, than any thus far projected.

It is interesting to compare the Citrohan house with Wright's Millard house in Pasadena, designed a year [or two] later. Note the similarity of the volume-concept of the interior, with the two-story living-area in front opening on a balcony, and the bedrooms and services on two levels behind. In 1931 it was hard to appreciate the originality in concept and in structure of the Millard house, because the patterned surface produced with the concrete blocks was so different from the smooth rendered surfaces which were still the sign-manual of the International Style, particularly as illustrated in the work of the Le Corbusier before 1930. Now, I think it is evident that such surface-patterning is a perfectly legitimate expression of the casting process by which Wright's blocks were made. Above all, 30 years have proved that patterned concrete surfaces, like Wright's of the 1920s, generally weather rather agreeably. The rendered surfaces of the early "International" buildings of the same period too often cracked and grew stained, thus losing all that quality of platonic abstraction which made them so striking.

> [Le Corbusier] was not the only innovator nor was the style as it came generally into being after 1922 peculiarly his own. He crystallized; he dramatized; but he was not alone in creating.

Le Corbusier was certainly a good deal responsible for there being a recognizable international style. Yet Gropius's work and the work of his pupils is doubtless more typical of the style; and he has always been an equally effective proponent, even if he does continue to disown the idea of style at every opportunity.

> It was in Mies's projects of 1922 that his true significance as an aesthetic innovator first appeared. In a design for a country house he broke with the conception of the wall as a continuous plane surrounding the plan and built up his composition of intersecting planes. Thus he achieved, still with the use of supporting walls, a greater openness even than Le Corbusier with his ferroconcrete skeleton construction.

Mies's country-house project of 1922, with its bearing walls of brick and its van Doesburg-like plan, seems even more significant today than it did twenty years ago. It very evidently does not fit either the principle of enclosed volume or the principle of regularity. (This serious critical dilemma seems hardly to have been noted in 1931.)

The next section of the book was concerned with "Functionalism." For in 1932 *The International Style* was conceived as a counterblast to functionalism, at least as we then understood that term.

> Some modern critics and groups of architects both in Europe and in America deny that the aesthetic element in architecture is important, or even that it exists. All aesthetic principles of style are to them meaningless and unreal.

There are still those who insist that architecture ought to be entirely a matter of technics and that architects should therefore hand over the whole field of building to engineers. But the glorification of engineering is a less popular critical gambit than it was earlier. (Then it will perhaps be recalled there was even a "Great Engineer" in the White House!) Yet, looking back over the building production of the last two generations, it is evident that the really great engineers have frequently built edifices which were more monumental and in many ways more visually effective than what most architects were able to achieve. The grain elevators of the Great Lakes ports stimulated Le Corbusier's ideas of what the new architecture might be like quite as much as did the "Tubism" of his friend the painter Léger. The engineer Freyssinet's hangar at Orly, of [1916], is still something that architects have been unable to rival for grandeur and clarity of form. The Goodyear Airship Dock at Akron is almost as impressive. What this really means is that some engineers are very good architects!

. . . [It is] nearly impossible to organize and execute a complicated building without making some choices not wholly determined by technics and economics. . . . Consciously or unconsciously the designer must make free choices before his design is completed.

Some sort of architectural style inevitably arises from the characteristic ways in which those free choices are made. Thus functionalism, even in the drastic terms of the Twenties, could have turned into a style, and to some Europeans it seems to have become one—the International Style, in fact! It is not necessary, of course, that engineers, or those architects who prefer to think of themselves as "pure" functionalists, should be able to explain in words their principles of design. (Some engineers at least, such as Arup and Samuely in England, can do so, however, and often very ably.)

. . . Critics should be articulate about problems of design; but architects, whose training is more technical than intellectual, can afford to be unconscious of the effects they produce. So, it may be assumed, were many of the great builders of the past.

As I have already noted, Mr. Johnson has given the most effective evidence of his own broad interpretation of the International Style in the buildings he has designed, rather than in writing. My own writing of the last 20 years, and perhaps particularly the book on Frank Lloyd Wright, *In the Nature of Materials* (1942), indicates—sometimes implicitly, sometimes explicitly—how my own ideas have been modified. It is worthwhile, none the less, to consider here a particular principle of the International Style as we saw it in 1932, notably the one concerning "Architecture as Volume." That was at best an ambiguous phrase, since volume is properly "contained space," while we were then chiefly concerned with the avoidance of effects of mass in the treatment of the exteriors of buildings.

Contemporary methods of construction provide a cage or skeleton of supports. Now the walls are merely subordinate elements fitted like screens between the supports or carried like a shell outside them.

The particular relationship of skeleton and shell which we then considered most characteristic of the International Style can best be illustrated, paradoxically, by the plan of a building that has never been accepted as representative of the style, Perret's church at LeRaincy, of 1923.

It is true that supporting wall sections are still sometimes used in combination with skeleton structure.

An early example of this, by one of the recognized leaders of the International Style, is illustrated in the plan of Le Corbusier's de Mandrot house of 1931. We considered that rather an exception. But today a very large number of modern American houses include (often quite arbitrarily it would seem) sections of supporting masonry, sometimes of brick, sometimes of rustic stonework, and very frequently of cinder or other concrete blocks introduced for effects of contrast and also because of their suitability in certain functional and structural situations. The idea may be abused but it can no longer be considered exceptional or reactionary.

The effect of mass, of static solidity, hitherto the prime quality of architecture, has all but disappeared; in its place there is an effect of volume, or more accurately, of surface planes bounding a volume. The prime architectural symbol is no longer the dense brick but the open box.

Certainly this statement is even truer, in a general way, than it was twenty years ago. Yet my fellow-author, Mr. Johnson, not only used a tower-like cylinder inside his house of glass in New Canaan, but contrasted the ultimate openness of the main house with a guest house of brick, almost as solid in appearance as if it had no interior whatsoever!

The most dramatic illustrations of the various methods of expressing interior skeletons still remain the American skyscrapers; but there are now rather more of them than there were in 1932, so that the character of their construction is better understood by the general public.

> The McGraw-Hill Building comes nearest to achieving aesthestically the expression of the enclosed steel cage, but it is still partially distorted into the old silhouette of a massive tower. . . . Yet the architect, Raymond Hood, in the Daily News Building which is in other ways less pure in expression, handled the setbacks so that they did not suggest steps and brought his building to a clean stop without decorative or terminal features.

It has too often been forgotten—and apparently was by us when writing in 1931—that long before Raymond Hood's day the Bayard or Conduit Building, of 1897, in New York, by Louis Sullivan, or better still his Gage Building, of the next year, at 18 South Michigan Avenue in Chicago, illustrated more clearly than Hood's skyscrapers, then newly completed, the proper architectural expression of steel-skeleton construction in the external cladding of a tall edifice. The later New York skyscrapers (and particularly those since the War that seem most literally to follow the precepts of the International Style in their design) are certainly not more expressive than these 50-year-old buildings. It is also interesting to note that Mies van der Rohe, in his Chicago apartment houses of the last few years, has moved closer and closer to Sullivan in the exterior treatment, whether the skeleton inside be of ferro-concrete or of steel. Even 20 years ago it was very difficult, apparently, to see the grandeur of the Sullivanian forest through the lush foliage of the ornament.

Style is character, style is expression; but even character must be displayed, and expression may be conscious and clear or muddled and deceptive. The architect who builds in the international style seeks to display the true character of his construction and to express clearly his provision for function. He prefers such an organization of his general composition, such a use of available surface materials, and such a handling of detail as will increase rather than contradict the prime effect of surface of volume.

The articulation of visible supports should also have been mentioned, whether isolated (as for example in the Johnson glass house or Mies's Farnsworth house on the Des Plaines river near Chicago) or actual sections of bearing wall (as in Le Corbusier's Le Pradet house or his [project for] Chile). A very striking example of vigorous articulation, in a quite sculptural way, of interior supports was in fact illustrated in the book—Aalto's Turun Sanomat Building at [Turku] in Finland, of 1930.

The flat roof was almost the sign-manual of the International Style in the early days. A loophole which proved very prophetic was left (fortunately) in the text on this subject:

Roofs with a single slant, however, have occasionally been used with success. Flat roofs are so much more useful that slanting or rounded roofs are only exceptionally justified.

The last sentence certainly represented a puristic and also a pseudofunctional position. But roofs are certainly of great importance in determining the character of the architecture of any period, particularly as regards small structures such as houses. Many architects have now swung so far from the belief that roofs must be flat that there is a tendency to over-exploit elaboration of the skyplane.

Since the roof was expected 20 years ago to be invisible, a great deal of space was given to the surfacing of exterior walls in the 1932 book.

> The spirit of the principle of [continuous] surface covers many exceptions to its letter. The type of construction represented by Mies van der Rohe's Barcelona pavilion, as well as that represented in Le Corbusier's house at Le Pradet, leads to a treatment of surfaces sensibly different from that which has been primarily stressed here.

Obviously these exceptions should have been a warning that the aesthetic "necessity" for the treatment of exterior walls as continuous surface was being much exaggerated. Curiously enough, California architects, working mostly with wood, have of late years been more faithful to the principle of continuity of surface than the European architects who were originally the most devoted to rendered and painted surfaces of cement.

The general statement with which this section concluded had its sound points:

The principle of surface of volume intelligently understood will always lead to special applications where the construction is not the typical cage or skeleton of supports surrounded by a protecting screen. The apparent exception may not prove the validity of the general principle, but it undoubtedly indicates its elasticity. Rigid rules of design are easily broken once and for all; elastic principles of architecture grow and flourish.

Rather than proceed with so detailed a commentary, it may be well to lead into a conclusion to this article by quoting a few of the more general remarks of 20 years ago which seem to remain valid still.

The second principle of contemporary style in architecture has to do with regularity. The supports in skeleton construction are normally and typically spaced at equal distances. Thus most buildings have an underlying regular rhythm which is clearly seen before the outside surfaces are applied. Moreover, economic considerations tend to favor the use of standardized parts throughout. Good modern architecture expresses in its design this characteristic orderliness of structure and this similarity of parts by an aesthetic ordering which emphasizes the underlying regularity. Bad modern design contradicts this regularity. Regularity is, however, relative and not absolute in architecture.
. . . the nearer approaches to absolute regularity are also approaches to monotony. . . . The principle of regularity refers to a means of organization, a way of giving definite form to an architectural design, rather than to an end which is sought for itself.
. . . The avoidance of symmetry should not be arbitrary or distorted.
. . . The mark of the bad modern architect is the positive cultiva-

tion of asymmetry for decorative reasons. For that can only be done in the majority of cases at the expense of common consistency and common sense. The mark of the good modern architect, on the other hand, is that the regularity of his designs approaches bilateral symmetry.

Exceptions to general rectangularity are only occasionally demanded by function and they may introduce complications in the regular skeleton of the structure. Non-rectangular shapes, particularly if they occur infrequently, introduce an aesthetic element of the highest positive interest. . . . They need seldom occur in ordinary building, but in monuments where the architect feels justified in seeking for a strongly personal expression, curves will be among the elements which give most surely extreme positive or negative aesthetic value. Curved and oblique forms seldom find a place in the cheapest solution of a given problem. But, if they can be afforded, they succeed, as they fail, on aesthetic grounds alone.

Aalto's Senior House at the Massachusetts Institute of Technology, of 1948, is obviously the most striking illustration of the increased use of curved and oblique forms. Whether most people approve of this prominent building or not, they tend to assume that Aalto was here consciously breaking with the rigidities of the International Style. Actually, as the paragraph above makes evident, even this notable post-War structure, though it may be at the extreme limit of the International Style as we understood it 20 years ago, is still in actual opposition to its sanctions only in the expressive irregularity of the plan and a few rather minor details, such as the willful roughness of the brickwork and the excessive clumsiness of some of the membering. Aalto was really reacting here, not against the International Style, but against that vulgar parodying of its more obvious aspects—the "Drugstore Modern"—which had become ubiquitous in the previous decade.

It was naturally to be expected, as the International Style became more widely accepted, that more and more weak and imitative architects would attempt to exploit its characteristic features. In 1932 we were amazingly optimistic and full of faith. We wrote:

> Anyone who follows the rules, who accepts the implications of an architecture that is not mass but volume, and who conforms to the principle of regularity can produce buildings which are at least aesthetically sound. If these principles seem more negative than positive, it is because architecture has suffered chiefly in the last century and a half from the extension of the sanctions of genius to all who have called themselves architects.

But it has not, of course, worked out that way. Many docile architects, and even builders outside the profession, have followed the rules dutifully enough, but their buildings can hardly be considered aesthetically sound. Doubtless the principles educed twenty years ago were too negative, and now we are ready, probably too ready, to extend the sanctions of genius very widely once more. If my tentative prognosis be correct, that we stand now at another change of phase in modern architecture between a "high" and a "late" period, we must expect many vagaries in reaction against the too literal interpretation of the International Style. We may also expect—and indeed already have with us—an academic current which is encouraging the repetition of established formulas without creative modulation. If the next 25 years are less disturbed by depressions and wars than the last have been, I suspect that our architecture will grow more diverse in kind. But I doubt if we will, for the next generation or more, lose contact altogether with the International Style, if that be interpreted as broadly as it was meant to be in 1932.

The International Style was not presented, in the 1932 book which first gave currency to the phrase, as a closed system; nor was it intended to be the whole of modern architecture, past, present, and future. Perhaps it has become convenient now to use the phrase chiefly to condemn the literal and unimaginative application of the design clichés of 25 years ago; if that is really the case, the term had better be forgotten. The "traditional architecture," which still bulked so large in 1932, is all but dead by now. The living architecture of the twentieth century may well be called merely "modern."

INDEX

INDICES

I. Architects

II. Countries